COLLECTORS' COMPENDIUM™ OF ROSEVILLE POTTERY

And Price Guide

Volume II

BANEDA
CREMONA
FERELLA
LAUREL
MONTACELLO
WINCRAFT

BY

RANDALL B. MONSEN

ISBN #0-9636102-6-0

This book is published by:

Monsen and Baer

Copyright © 1997

All Rights Reserved

ISBN #0-9636102-6-0

Individual copies of this book
may be ordered for $45 each directly from:

[Wholesale inquiries are also invited]

Monsen and Baer
Box 529
Vienna, VA 22183 USA

Telephone: [703] 938-2129
FAX: [703] 242-1357

COLLECTORS' COMPENDIUM™ **OF ROSEVILLE POTTERY**

Volume I

Artcraft - Artwood - Cosmos - Earlam - Falline - Futura

BY **RANDALL B. MONSEN**

Volume I is also available for $35 from Monsen and Baer

CONTENTS

Dedication

This book is dedicated to R. L. B.,
a partner in the truest sense of the word.

Collectors' Compendium of Roseville Pottery
Volume II

Preface

The publication of the first volume of the Roseville Compendium was one of the most rewarding experiences Rodney Baer and I have had during the entire time we have collected Roseville Pottery. The first volume of the Roseville Compendium, published in May, 1995, turned out to be highly successful from a publishing point of view, and I hope also from a scholarly and research point of view. Several major antique journals and newspapers carried very favorable reviews, which greatly helped the sale of the book, as did the numerous enthusiastic reactions from collectors who bought the book, read it, and then told their fellow collectors about it. Most important to me was the positive feedback and encouraging words I received from other collectors and dealers, and many have written us to tell us about unusual pieces of pottery they have found, or of historical references that were previously unknown to us, or just simply that they liked the book in general. Each of these comments was very much appreciated. As early as the fall of 1995, I became eager to begin work on Volume II. However, part of the difficulty in undertaking a second volume of the Compendium has always been the need to find all the pieces of the patterns which we wished to document. Even for those Roseville lines that are not considered particularly rare [such as those of the 1940's], it is not at all easy to find each and *every* piece of any single line. Inevitably there are one or two pieces, sometimes a grand jardiniere and pedestal but more often merely a humble console bowl, that prove elusive. Anyone who would doubt this should attempt to do it. And in the case of the middle period lines, assembling all the pieces is a doubly difficult task. First, one must locate the pots but then also be able to afford to purchase them, and in today's marketplace both of these things can be equally difficult.

What is a compendium? A compendium is a comprehensive and exhaustive inventory or summary of a topic. The keynote of a compendium is its comprehensiveness, and that is why we undertake to describe only some Roseville lines in each volume. Many previously published books have given examples of Roseville pottery, so there would be no point in merely doing that. What we wanted to provide for collectors in the *Collectors' Compendium of Roseville Pottery* is a comprehensive treatment and catalogue of each of the lines we write about. Our purpose is to enrich collecting by sharing our knowledge of Roseville pottery. Documenting all the different shapes in each line [and the colors and glazes with which they could be decorated] is an integral part of our purpose. Providing price-guide information is also a part of that purpose. In the first volume of this *Roseville Compendium*, we described: Futura, Falline, Artcraft, Earlam, Cosmos, and Artwood. This second volume continues with presentations of: Baneda, Cremona, Ferella, Laurel, Montacello, and Wincraft. All of the pieces seen in this book, except where specifically noted, are from the Monsen and Baer collection. We intend to continue this mammoth undertaking with Volume III. One pattern that we have been attempting to complete is Imperial II. While it is not difficult to find some examples of Imperial II, finding all of them is extremely difficult, and we are still actively seeking the shapes #480-8 and #483-10. We would be delighted to purchase these pieces, if anyone can locate them for us. Volume III of the Compendium will document still other lines, and in general we would like to produce a successive new volume on an annual basis. The publication of each Volume will be accompanied by an update on the price-guide evaluation of previous volumes.

While we attempt to be complete in our discussion, photographs, and listings for each of the pottery lines we include, it will inevitably be the case nonetheless that new pots, or pots with novel decorations and colors come to light after the publication of this book. Learning and research are gradual processes that do not come to an abrupt halt because of the mere publication of a book, and so completeness of coverage is, in actuality, a goal more than an achievement. Therefore, new information, as it becomes available, will be incorporated into second editions of the book. We have tried never to be dogmatic about what does not exist, but rather to describe the pots we have seen and observed. We have generally collected Roseville with a strong preference for one specific color in which it was produced, for example, the Baneda pattern decorated in green, Orian in red, and Falline in blue and green. For the *Roseville Compendium*, our objective is to show photographs of all of the different shapes in a given pattern, as well as some representative examples of pots decorated in the different colors in which each line was produced. But we do not think it is necessary to show each shape in each of the different color patterns, and we will not attempt to do that, either in this book or in subsequent ones. Any piece of Roseville pottery can be unambiguously identified by referring to its Roseville mold number, together with a specification of which color pattern was used to decorate it.

The continuation of our research on Roseville pottery was done with the help of many people. I would like to express my sincere gratitude to the children of Frank Barks, that is, to Bill Barks, Judy Wahl, Pat Hupp, and Francis 'Hank' Barks. Frank Barks left with his children the legacy of a loving and caring father, and I am happy in this book to have been able to give him the credit he richly deserves for his important role, only poorly understood until now, in the creation of Roseville pottery. Mr. Gene Menhorn, employed at the Roseville factory in the 1940's, was also very helpful. Dan Veirs continues to give me encouragement as well as helpful information about two Roseville patterns in which we both share a keen interest: Carnelian and Imperial II. Ken Forster, with his extensive knowledge of American art pottery, has shared many useful thoughts. I would also like to thank Charlie Kearns, who knows and loves Zanesville and its artistic heritage, Dr. Phillip A. LaDouceur, Mrs. Gene Ridgely, Tim Onstatt and Dr. Charles Dietz. I would also like to thank Curt Rustand, Greg Koster, and Gordon Hoppe for allowing pieces from their collections to be shown in this book.

The past gives up its secrets so reluctantly. Still in all, searching for new information does produce some results, as can be seen in this volume, and we will continue to do it. We are still very much interested in finding out more information about Frank Ferrell, the designer of Roseville pottery of the period from at least 1918 onward. Since the publication of Volume I, much more information and many more documents and photographs have come to light, and we include what we have found in this volume. If you have more information about Frank Ferrell, or if you have unusual pieces of Roseville pottery that we may not have seen [such as trial glazes, experimentals, unusual shapes], please contact us. The experimental and trial glaze pieces are quite important, because they shed light upon relations of one line to another, and upon the process leading to the creation of the pottery. Sometimes the pottery itself can reveal to us what no human and no document can tell.

This long and wonderful journey into American art pottery which has culminated in the publication of these volumes of the Roseville Compendium, began simply enough with the purchase of some Roseville pots in the early 1980's. The beauty of the pottery itself led me to seek the history of the company that produced it and the designer who conceived it. It was in this way that I was led to search out the details of the life of Frank Ferrell, but in some ways it seems more that he found me rather than the other way around. Our pottery collection now includes much Peters and Reed, Weller, and Owens pottery, in addition to Roseville. How and when and with what resources we will be able to complete this enormous project of collecting and documentation we truly do not know and cannot as yet even guess, but we will continue to attempt to do it. We are very grateful to other pottery collectors who have encouraged and supported this endeavor.

Randall B. Monsen
Rodney L. Baer   May 30, 1997.

The Roseville Pottery

The Roseville Pottery Company was among the most commercially successful of all the enterprises which produced art pottery for American consumers during the late nineteenth and early-to-mid twentieth centuries. It provided a livelihood for hundreds of workers over many decades, and greatly enriched its owners; today it seemingly continues to provide a livelihood for many antique dealers, and it may well continue to do so for a very long time yet to come. The Roseville Pottery existed for a span of 64 years only, from 1890 to December 12, 1954. During this time, Roseville produced and sold uncountable millions of pottery vessels of every sort imaginable, from humble utilitarian flower pots to superbly designed and beautifully executed art pottery which will be cherished for its beauty ever more greatly by each new generation of collectors and admirers who fall under its charm.

The history of the Roseville Pottery can be divided rather sharply into two parts. For the first 28 years, essentially the period from its founding in 1890 to 1918, the company produced both utilitarian items such as jardinieres and kitchen pitchers as well as more artistic hand-painted or hand-decorated lines of pottery such as Rozane, Olympic, Mongol, Mostique, Aztec, Donatello and Della Robbia. The Roseville Pottery profited during this period from the artistic talents of Frederick and Harry Rhead, from glazes developed by J. Herold, and from the artistic handwork of many known and unknown artists who both decorated and executed the pottery. The major American art pottery enterprises—including Roseville, Weller, and Rookwood [but not limited to them]—all produced lines of pottery to compete with each other, with the result that there are many stylistic and technical similarities between them. In this sense, the Standard Glaze pottery of Rookwood is very similar in appearance to Rozane of Roseville and Louwelsa of Weller. These similarities are so strong that in some cases even experienced collectors would hesitate to identify one of the three without inspecting the bottom for identifying marks. The Fairfield line of Weller bears a striking similarity to Donatello of Roseville [to the extent that some collectors confuse the two]; the Eocean ware line of Weller was apparently marketed to compete with the Iris glaze pots of Rookwood, and many additional examples could be given to illustrate this point. The reasons for these artistic similarities have been discussed by other authors [e. g., Henzke, 1982], and they have as much to do with the fact that many of the same individuals went to work at each different pottery company as they have to do with simple marketplace competition among companies producing the same kind of product. To be sure, the similarities among the Zanesville potteries are possibly the greatest. This first period of Roseville, from 1890 to 1918 is

very different from the second part, from 1918 to 1954.

The year 1918 was a major turning point for the Roseville Pottery, because of many changes which occurred in that year or very near to it. The most important of these changes is that in 1918, Frank L. D. Ferrell came to work at Roseville and assumed the position of Art Director; it is possible nonetheless that he may have submitted pottery designs to Roseville before that time. In 1918, George Young, the President and founder of the company, retired, and the position of President of the Roseville Pottery was assumed by his son, Russell Young. George Krause, responsible for the fine glazes used on Roseville pottery, also had just come to work there in 1917. In addition, Frank Barks began to work at Roseville probably in 1918. Thus, from around 1918 onward, many of the stylistic similarities between Roseville pottery and other American art pottery begin to diminish probably in largest part because Ferrell was a highly original designer, not a mere imitator of others' works. Ferrell worked at Roseville for the next 36 years, and he designed there thousands of different pottery vessels and in so doing he defined the artistic direction of the company. For the Roseville Pottery, these thirty-six years were more than half its entire existence; for Frank Ferrell, these years represented the last half of his long and very distinguished career. Ferrell designed lines of pottery for Roseville each containing dozens of different shapes, and this pottery was as popular among consumers of the time as it is now among collectors on the secondary antique market. The commercial viability of these Ferrell-designed lines [of which the Pinecone line may be the best known example and the greatest commercial success] buoyantly supported the Roseville Pottery as a business throughout the Great Depression; the Herculean difficulty of accomplishing this economic miracle of marketing non-essential artware during the Depression can be easily overlooked in our present, prosperous times, but we can grasp it better when we reflect that the Weller Pottery closed in 1948; Rookwood entered bankruptcy in 1941. Roseville, in contrast, survived until 1954. Contrary to what has been written in some published sources, the Ferrell period of Roseville, from 1918 to 1954, was in fact a period of Roseville's finest artistic triumphs—exactly the opposite of the impression one gets from reading many of the erudite books on American art pottery. As time passes, this fact will become clearer and clearer, and eventually it will become impossible to ignore or to deny it.

During the early part of the Ferrell era of Roseville, several different lines of pottery were produced in some years, and at least two different new lines in other years. In many of the Depression years, four or more lines were produced each year. Later, two new lines of pottery were introduced regularly each year, one in January and one in July. In some years, employees were laid off during the period between production of the lines in May and June, depending on the volume of production [Menhorn Interview, 1996]. Generally, a line was produced for at least two years after its introduction. [Pinecone was produced for a much longer period, of course.] As a result, about six different lines would be available to retailers at any one time, although for very large commissioned orders, the company would in some cases produce lines which were technically out of production. For example, a price list for January 1954 shows prices for assorted Sand Jars, Pinecone II, Capri, and Floraline. At present, we believe that Ferrell designed the following catalogue of lines. A similar list was published in

Figure 1. An aerial photograph of the Roseville factory on Linden Avenue. The Muskingum River can be seen in the lower right of the photo, and railroad tracks can be seen along the river. This photograph was probably taken in the 1940's. The factory itself occupied three distinct long buildings, each situated parallel and very close to the others. The building with the black roof housed the business offices and showroom. The middle building housed the kilns, and the third building was used for Ferrell's and Barks' studio and as a warehouse for finished pottery. Just where Linden Avenue curves to the left as one is headed away from Zanesville, there can be seen a loading dock that was a part of this last building. That loading dock still remains today, and it is the only part of the original Roseville factory that does. ***Every piece of Roseville pottery in the hands of collectors today at one time passed across the threshold of that loading dock.*** Just north of the main factory complex is a smaller separate building, called the straw shed. A special straw shed was needed because of the very large volume of straw consumed when the pottery was packed for shipment, and the straw shed was the source of at least one major fire. The two small sheds perpendicular to one another at the south end of the factory [near a parking lot for cars] were used to store old molds.

Volume I, and some of the dates are corrected here. We have added some lines; note in particular Futura Carnelian and Crystal Green [= Laurel Branch]. There are still some unresolvable inconsistencies in the dating of these lines inventoried below, so this list is subject to future correction and emendation. At the present time, this list extends to *ninety-six* different pottery lines.

Frank Ferrell Roseville Lines:

Sylvan, 1918
Cremo, 191-
Vista, 191-
Dogwood I, 1918
Velmoss Scroll, 1918
Volpato, 1919
Panel, 1920
Florane, 1920's
Lustre, 1921
Azurine, Orchid, Turquoise, 1921
Corinthian, 1923
La Rose [Garland], 1924
Hexagon, 1924
Imperial I, 1924
Rosecraft Vintage, 1924
Dogwood II, 1924
Dahlrose, 1924
Florentine, 1924
Victorian Art Pottery, 1924
Normandy, 1924
Lombardy, 1924
Tuscany, 1926
Cremona, 1927
Carnelian I, 1927
Carnelian II, 1927
Savona, 1927
Futura, 1928
Futura Carnelian, 1929
Imperial II, 1929
Earlam, 1930
Ferella, 1930
Sunflower, 1930
Rosecraft colors 1930's
Matt colors 1930's
Florane, 1931
Jonquil, 1931
Windsor, 1931
Montacello, 1931
Cherry Blossom, 1932
Baneda, 1932
Falline, 1932
Ivory, 1932
Tourmaline, 1932
Wisteria, 1932
Ixia, 1933
Blackberry, 1933
Artcraft, 1934
Clemana, 1934

Laurel, 1934
Topeo, 1934
Luffa, 1934
Russco, 1934
Pinecone, 1935
Velmoss, 1935
Morning Glory, 1935
Orian, 1935
Clemana, 1936
Primrose, 1936
Moderne, 1936
Moss, 1936
Teasel, 1936
Thorn Apple, 1937
Dawn, 1937
Poppy, 1938
Fuschia, 1938
Iris, 1939
Cosmos, 1939
Crystal Green, 1939
Bleeding Heart, 1940
White Rose, 1940
Rozane, 1941
Columbine, 1941
Bushberry, 1941
Foxglove, 1942
Peony, 1942
Water Lily, 1943
Magnolia, 1943
Clematis, 1944
Freesia, 1945
Zephyr Lily, 1946
Snowberry, 1947
Wincraft, 1948
Apple Blossom, 1948
Ming Tree, 1949
Capri/Mayfair, 1949
Gardenia, 1950
Burmese, 1950
Silhouette, 1950
Mock Orange, 1950
Bittersweet, 1951
Floraline, 1951
Artwood, 1951
Lotus, 1951
Florane, 1951
Pasadena, 1953
Pinecone II, 1953

For many decades of its existence, the Roseville Pottery advertised its pottery in popular magazines. Examples of these advertisements were shown in Volume I of the Compendium. These ads tended to follow a specific formula. First, an attractive photograph of some of the pottery was shown; often the vases contained some flowers or branches, but usually not a full bouquet. When flowers were used to show the function of the vessels, they usually had the spare appearance similar to Japanese ikebana—often merely a branch of cherry blossoms or bittersweet. The picture was often followed by a quote about beauty,

ZANESVILLE, OHIO, U.S.A.

Figure 2. A promotional booklet published by the Roseville Pottery. In magazine ads of the time, readers were urged to "write for a free booklet." Those who did received this. This example bears a copyright date of 1931, and the lines advertised inside are: Bushberry, Rozane, Columbine, White Rose, and Bleeding Heart.

The Oldest of the Arts

THE origin of pottery is cloaked in the dim mists of the far past. It was the idea of no particular race or place, but arose from the necessities of life everywhere as man progressed toward civilization. It is thus the oldest of the arts, starting long before written records were made.

Just how pottery originated is, then, a matter of conjecture, but it is believed that, in his groping way, man, after a long time, noticed that clay could be shaped and hardened and that fire increased its hardness. The idea came to him slowly, perhaps, from seeing holes in clay soil retain water, or from the nests of birds lined with clay. In some way, at any rate, primitive man conceived the thought of fashioning vessels from clay. He found first of all that these were valuable for cooking and for keeping food and water. Later they adorned his dwellings.

Reaching back to the days before civilization began, pottery enables us to follow more closely the history of the human race than does any other art. It tells us of the hopes and aspirations of mankind through the ages, showing in an intriguing manner a constant effort for greater comfort and beauty in life.

The story of pottery is a romantic one and takes in all ages, all lands and all climates. The high points of the story are here given for all who may be interested in it and who seek a better understanding of modern creations as represented for example, by ROSEVILLE pottery.

Egypt. Predynastic jar decorated with gazelles and ostriches.

The Potter's Wheel

MAN shaped crude vessels of clay by hand and baked them in the sun. After time had elapsed he learned to construct rude kilns in which to bake his creations of clay. Then, by some stroke of genius, the potter's wheel was invented. How long ago is not known, but it was one of the very first mechanical devices and was highly regarded by ancient peoples. Both the Egyptians and the Chinese claim its invention. It was the first revolutionary step in the world of art.

Figures 3 and 4. Pages three and part of page four from the booklet *Roseville*.

The Tombs of Greece

LIKE many other ancient peoples, the Greeks placed articles in the tombs of their dead, which they believed the departed would use in the other world. From these tombs have been unearthed a wealth of beautiful vases and jars showing the skill of the Greeks in pottery.

March Through Europe

THE making of pottery in artistic decorative forms now spread rapidly through the various countries of Europe. The European artist potters were largely on their own. The works of ancient Egypt, Greece and Rome were as yet practically unknown. They worked out their own designs and methods of production. Examples coming through from China served to spur them on.

West of the Atlantic

IN the Americas, the Indians had learned to make pottery of a crude nature before the discovery by Columbus. Some of the best examples of present-day Indian pottery are found among the Navajos.

Figures 5-9. Parts of pages five, six, nine, ten, and all of page eleven from the booklet *Roseville*.

The Chinese Masters

THE Chinese were highly skilled in making products from clay and claim an antiquity in this art as old as that of Egypt. Examples that have been found seem to substantiate their claims. They were the first to invent porcelain, in which they were no doubt assisted by the presence of great beds of kaolin, a fine white clay.

and Then ... ROSEVILLE

BUILDING on the progress made in the art of pottery through the centuries, decorative and ornamental pottery of high quality, charming designs and true artistic value are created at Zanesville, Ohio, by the Roseville Pottery, Inc.

Established December 8, 1890, the Roseville Pottery, Inc., has been continuously under the same management. The craftsmen who produce ROSEVILLE creations have devoted a life-time to their art. The enthusiasm and loyalty they have for their chosen work is reflected in the loving care, profound skill and originality of conception which distinguish ROSEVILLE pottery.

The opinion authorities have of ROSEVILLE pottery can be seen in this quotation from the Encyclopedia Americana (Vol. 22, page 457):

"At Zanesville, Ohio, a large quantity of ornamental pottery is made, the best of which is the multi-colored glazes of the Roseville Pottery, Inc., extraordinary in the beauty of their color and challenging comparison with some of the best examples of Oriental art."

The art of pottery is the union of two branches of art, the architectural and the graphic. It combines form and proportion with drawing and color.

"The entire vitality of art depends upon its being either full of truth or full of use," says Ruskin. "It must state a true thing or adorn a useful one." ROSEVILLE pottery does both. It meets all the requirements of what is right in ceramic art to the entire satisfaction of good judges, thus placing it at once among the finest potteries of the age.

Worthy indeed to be counted among your most cherished possessions are the superb creations of the Roseville potteries. For more than three decades they have been the delight of those who love and appreciate beautiful things.

or the importance of beauty in the home, and then there was some ad copy text about Roseville pottery. Finally, the reader was invited to send for a "free booklet" on Roseville. These booklets were produced over a very broad span of time, from the 1920's through the 1940's; many of them have survived and today are highly collectable themselves. An important thing to notice is that the copyright date of each booklet is typically very different from the production date of the pottery promoted in each of the booklets. For example, a booklet bearing *Copyright 1931* on the inside cover was used to advertise Bleeding Heart, Bushberry, Rozane, and Columbine, which were of course produced more than a decade later, in the 1940's. It is not correct that the copyright date of the booklet is equal to the production date of the pottery advertised inside it.

An example of part of one of these booklets is given here. The idea that Roseville wanted to convey is essentially quite valid and clear: that the history of human art is most easily documented in a continuous fashion by looking at pottery. "Reaching back to the days before civilization began, pottery enables us to follow more closely the history of the human race than does any other art. It tells us of the hopes and aspirations of mankind through the ages, showing in an intriguing manner a constant effort for greater comfort and beauty in life." The booklet would then give examples of art pottery throughout history: Ancient Egypt, Greece, Rome, China, Europe, American Indian pottery. Only then would this booklet introduce Roseville, and it did so by showing it as the modern example of the same kind of art pottery as produced in other civilizations in other epochs. On page 11 of one such booklet, the heading begins: "And Then.....Roseville." The text points out on this page eleven of the booklet:

"Building on the progress made in the art of pottery through the centuries, decorative and ornamental pottery of high quality, charming designs, and true artistic value are created at Zanesville, Ohio, by the Roseville Pottery, Inc. .... The art of pottery is the union of two branches of art, the architectural and the graphic. It combines form and proportion with drawing and color. 'The entire vitality of art depends upon its being either full of truth or full of use,' says Ruskin. 'It must state a true thing or adorn a useful one.' Roseville pottery does both. It meets all the requirements of what is right in ceramic art to the entire satisfaction of good judges, thus placing it at once among the finest potteries of the age. Worthy indeed to be counted among your most cherished possessions are the superb creations of the Roseville potteries. For more than three decades they have been the delight of those who love and appreciate beautiful things."

It is clear from the above, as well as from many other sources, that beauty alone, far and above mere function, was the defining trait of Roseville pottery. In the truest sense of the word, then, Roseville pottery is indeed art pottery. But Roseville pottery was intended for the average citizen. It was something anyone could buy as a wedding present or a birthday gift. And the American public did buy it, for a long time and in vast quantities. During the 1930's, Roseville pottery was very often given proudly as a wedding gift, much as one might give silver or a modern appliance today.

From its beginning to its end, the Roseville Pottery Company was a family-owned and managed enterprise. There were originally, at its incorporation, 1000 shares of stock. At the 1996 Rookwood and Keramics VI auction in Cincinnati, some of these stock shares, now "worthless" of course, were entered as lots; when auctioned, they were anything but worthless. The author purchased one of the stock certificates to illustrate in this book. It is shown in Figure 15. Of the original 1000 Roseville shares, 998 of them descended to Anna Mae Young upon the death of her father George Young. For reasons ostensibly having to do with corporate law, one share each was owned by lawyers who sat on the Board of Directors. This particular one share, originally owned by E. R. Meyers, was transferred in December 30, 1940, to Fenwick Scott Clement and was further transferred in 1944 to Leota Young Clement. The 998 shares of stock originally owned by Anna Mae Young were divided among her daughters Leota Young and Anna Young as well as to other descendants. Upon the death of Anna Mae Young, the presidency of the Roseville pottery descended always through sons-in-law: first, in 1937, to Fenwick Scott Clement, and then, in 1944, to Clement's son-in-law, Robert Windisch, who remained at the head of it until the company ceased operations. At the Ohio Historical Library one can read about the final shareholders' meetings, but it is truly rather sad reading and reveals little more than various groups of relatives forming factions to oppose each other, and all to little avail. A business failure, especially of a grand company such as this, is a pathetic spectacle indeed.

About Frank Ferrell

Frank L. D. Ferrell spent his entire long career, from about 1894 to 1954—six whole decades—working in the field of American art pottery. He was born in Zanesville on May 22, 1878, a child of Charles H. and Elizabeth Ailes Ferrell. It was in Zanesville where he also died 83 years later, of congestive heart failure, on August 10, 1961. It is uncertain whether Ferrell had any formal art training, but it is unlikely that

he had much of it, at least in the academic sense. He did, however, study under the tutelage of Karl Kappes. Karl Kappes worked as an artist for the Weller Pottery. At that time there was a Zanesville Art Club, formed by employees of the local potteries. It is probable that Ferrell also received some informal training at this club—or more likely, *he may have trained others*. Like Kappes, Ferrell also apparently began working with

Figure 10. A very rare photograph of Frank Ferrell taken inside the Roseville factory, quite possibly in his studio where he created Roseville designs. At this time Ferrell was at the prime of his career. See Figure 11 for a close-up photo of the calendar, vase, and plaque on the wall. The year was 1925; the photographer was possibly Frank Barks. This photo was given to the author by William Barks.

Figure 11. A close-up photo part of Figure 10. Note the calendar, vase, and plaque on the wall. The year was 1925, the month either September, November, or December; both the plaque and the vase [Moss Aztec?] on the wall are unidentified.

art and design rather than in business management. But yet he must have had a keen sense not only of what would make for an artful and pleasing design in pottery, and, equally [or more] important, what would capture the imagination of the public—in a word, what would sell. Whatever we want to call that kind of intuition, it is certainly related to business acumen. That kind of intuition was never common. In addition, Ferrell was undoubtedly not an assertive man, a fact verified by interviews with many people in Zanesville who knew him. In contrast, George Krause, who developed many of Roseville's wonderful lustrous glaze formulas, did manage to get a seat on the Board of Directors, which must not have been easy since he was totally unrelated to the Young, Clement, or Windisch families. But Ferrell remained in the same position he held when he joined the company in 1918.

The obituary of Frank Ferrell published in the *Zanesville Times Recorder* used a spelling of his name as Ferrel, and it is found spelled that way also in other published sources; his death certificate likewise uses the one 'l' spelling. Among the sparse facts stated in the obituary are these: "Mr. Ferrel [*sic* in this instance, and hereafter] was long a member of the Coburn Methodist Church and Lafayette Lodge No. 79, F. & A. M. He was also a member of the Timber Run Grange. [...] His only sister, Mrs. Anna Earich died in 1934. Mr. Ferrel was never married. Mr. Ferrel had been associated with Roseville Pottery for nearly 40 years and prior to that had been employed as a designer for the Weller Pottery. He was one of the leading pottery designers in the nation. His creations became well known all over the world and in recent years have been copied by many other firms, attesting to their universal appeal. Many of his original designs were considered by potterymen to be "Ferrel trademarks" and over the years he reworked the most popular ones into new and interesting lines of pottery ware to keep abreast of modern trends. He was active in various sports in his earlier years and was a sponsor of Zanesville girls' softball teams for many years. The Rev. Ray Bird, assistant pastor of the Coburn Methodist Church will officiate and burial will follow in Greenwood Cemetery."

The spelling of Ferrell's name as *Ferrel*—with only one *l*—in many published sources such as the

the Weller Company, as an artist on the Louwelsa line, until 1905; at what year he began is uncertain, but it probably was 1894 or even earlier, when he would have been merely sixteen years old. He was obviously a child prodigy—a fact that was probably very evident then [to people such as Samuel Weller], but which has by now been forgotten. By the time Ferrell began working for Roseville, he already had twenty-five years professional experience working in American art pottery. The importance of this fact is that when he began working at Roseville in 1918, Ferrell was in the prime of his creative life.

Frank Ferrell was never a shareholder of the Roseville Company, nor was he ever even a member of the Board of Directors. This would not have seemed unusual given the fact that his talents were clearly in

Figure 12. An official photograph of the Roseville Pottery on the occasion of its 50th anniversary, on December 7, 1940. Frank Ferrell is at the very center in the back row. This was a gala event at the time, and it was written up days before and days after in the *Zanesville Times Recorder*. Guests were served a seven-course banquet, followed by a stage show with fifteen acts, and dancing to music by Red Norvo and his band. See the enlargement in Fig. 13; photo courtesy of Elvin Culp.

above obituary had long been a vexing riddle to the author. In *Volume I* of the *Compendium* and in this book I have used the spelling with two final l's because that is the way he himself spelled his name when he signed it on vases, and there are many such examples of his signature. I reasoned that he could not have been wrong about the spelling of his own name. Yet it perplexed me greatly that his death certificate has his name unmistakably spelled *Ferrel*. In the summer of 1996, while attending the Zanesville Pottery Festival, I ventured one day into the old Greenwood Cemetery, without so much as a clue as to where Frank Ferrell's grave might be located, and knowing only [from his published obituary] that it must be there somewhere. Wandering about this peaceful old cemetery which lies between the roaring interstate highway 70 on the one side and the placid old highway 40 on the other, I somehow managed to come upon Frank Ferrell's grave. To my great surprise, his headstone, as well as that of his mother and father, have the family name clearly marked Ferrel. This finally explains the problematic spelling. His family name was indeed Ferrel, but he chose a slightly more artistic spelling of it for his career as an artist. Both, then, are correct *in a sense*. I have decided to maintain the spelling as Ferrell, since that is how he himself designated it in his life as a designer of pottery, and this book is about that persona.

There are six graves all together in a row for the Ferrel family, given here in the same order from left to right that they are to be found in the cemetery itself: Charles H. Ferrel [1848-1908] and Elizabeth F.

Ferrel [1850-1942]; Frank L. Ferrel [1878-1961]; Edith M. Earich [Frank F.'s niece, 1893-1968]; Anna I. Earich [Frank F.'s sister, 1871-1934]; Austin E. Earich [Anna Earich's husband, 1870-1958]. Frank Ferrell never married and had no children, and the only child of Anna [Frank Ferrell's sister] and Austin Earich was Edith Earich, who also never married. Thus, the entire immediate family came to an end when Edith Earich died in 1968. At the time that Frank Ferrell died, he had been living in a trailer on the west side of Zanesville. His niece, Edith Earich, and her close personal friend, Mrs. Glen Ridgely, cleaned the trailer out. Edith Earich then inherited the trailer and she had it moved into town and subsequently lived in it until her death in 1968. Somewhere among family mementos, Mrs. Ridgely located a tiny photo taken very early in Frank Ferrell's career. This extraordinary and important photograph, considerably enlarged, is shown here [Figure 16]. An enlargement of this photograph is now also on display at the Zanesville Art Center along side the actual vase shown in the photograph.

This photograph shows a very different Frank Ferrell than anyone had seen heretofore. He is very young, at the beginning of his career, with piercing eyes and dark black hair, and dressed for the photographer as an artist. Samuel Weller had selected Frank Ferrell to decorate his most important and his largest creations for the St. Louis World's Fair of 1904, called the Louisiana Purchase Exposition. The Fair had originally been scheduled for 1903 to coincide with the centennial of the Louisiana Purchase, but was delayed a year

Figure 13. A close-up of the official photograph of the Roseville Pottery on the occasion of its 50th anniversary, on December 7, 1940. Frank Ferrell is seated at the very center in the back row. Since there is no dining table there, it is quite possible that he, as well as those others standing along the back, had been actually seated at the tables on the far right of the photo, and would have thus moved there for the occasion at the direction of the photographer. The tables appear to have floral arrangements in Roseville vases of the Russco pattern. Photo courtesy of Elvin Culp.

due to construction problems. Ferrell is pictured with one of the large vases beautifully decorated with irises. It is a spectacular piece of American art pottery. This vase now permanently resides in the Zanesville Art Center for all to see. Since this vase must have been completed well in advance of 1904, we might assume that the date of this photograph is about 1900. An even larger vase decorated by Ferrell for the same event in the Aurelian pattern, had been completed even earlier, in 1897. Recall that Ferrell was born in 1878, and that he was therefore possibly as young as twenty years old when this photo had been taken. In all probability, he may have started to work for Weller by age 15 or even earlier. Thus, he was in reality still a teenager when he completed the St Louis World's Fair Aurelian vase, since we know it was completed by 1897.

The people who knew Frank Ferrell personally recall many different facts about him. He was very active in the Timber Run Grange. The Grange was an important institution in rural America, and it provided not only social occasions but membership also allowed one to purchase insurance. The importance of insurance cannot be overemphasized, since in the early twentieth century it was not provided by employers. Many people have mentioned that Ferrell liked horses, golfing, fishing, opera, and especially photography. Some of the photographs shown here attest to these pursuits. He apparently also played at polo, quite surprisingly, since such sport was far from common in Midwest America then or even now. Ferrell developed a close personal friendship with Frank Barks and his whole family, a friendship which spanned four decades. Ferrell and Barks shared many interests, including the opera and photography. Apparently Ferrell took many photographs of people and places in Zanesville, but in all likelihood it may sadly be the case that these photographs were discarded after his death.

A banquet photograph of the Roseville Pottery's 50th anniversary party provides an interesting glimpse at the people who created the pottery we now love to collect. This banquet was held in the Rogge Hotel in Zanesville on December 7, 1940, and it must certainly have been one of the most important social occasions of the time. We have not yet identified many

of the people in this photograph, and we are unable to identify Frank Barks. Careful scrutiny of this photo shows that there were flowers placed on all the tables, and quite appropriately enough, these flowers appear to have been placed *in* Roseville pottery, probably cornucopias of the Russco or Ivory pattern. There appears to be one main room with some seated at large round tables or at smaller square ones. In the background, one can see that there was an adjoining room with additional seating for others at long tables. Obviously, the seating must have reflected to some extent the individual's importance in the company. The important men appear to be seated in the foreground at a large round table, whereas the more important women appear to be seated at a similar table next to them. A long line of people standing near the left rear appear to have been sitting for the banquet near the

Figure 14. The largest piece of American art pottery, decorated by Frank Ferrell for the Weller Pottery, as depicted on a popular tourist postcard from Zanesville. This vase was sold on May 16, 1997 at Skinners Auction in Boston at a price of $115,000.00.

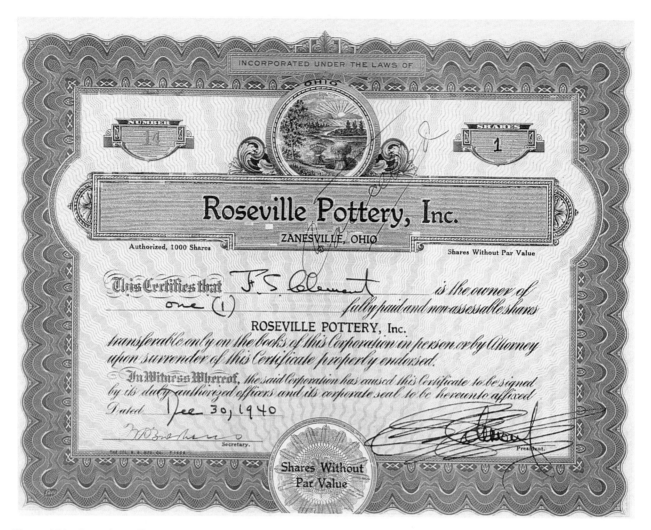

Figure 15A. A stock certificate for one share of the Roseville Pottery. This one share originally belonged to Fenwick Clement, and then to Leota Young Clement; the record of transfer shown in Figure 15B is signed by Robert Windisch, after whom the Wincraft pattern of Roseville was named.

far right hand side of the room, and were undoubtedly asked to move from there to the back so that they could be included in the photograph. The photographer must have been clever, since it could not have been technically easy to include all in the picture.

And where then is Frank Ferrell, the man without whose artistic talents probably none of them would have been sitting down to enjoy a banquet? He is almost exactly where one might expect, in the far distant background but yet at the very dead center. We have enlarged that section of the photo to clearly show his face. We cannot help but wonder if he was acknowledged in some manner at this banquet. Probably a program for this banquet might exist, but if one of them has survived, it is at present unknown to us. Following the seven-course banquet, there was a floor show with fifteen acts to it, and dancing was accompanied by Red Norvo and his orchestra. According to the *Zanesville Times Recorder* report of the banquet in their December 9, 1940 issue: "The high spot of the

evening was reached when Mr. Clement [President of the Company] presented awards in the form of checks in the amount of one dollar for each year of service to all those employed at the company for 25 years or more. Wade France, head of the shipping department, received a check for $42." As far as can be determined, Frank Ferrell would by then have been at Roseville for only 22 years, and thus would not have received a check [...for $22].

Frank Ferrell's talents were keenly appreciated by the owners of the four major potteries where he worked: Weller, Owens, Peters and Reed, and Roseville. In the present-day world of art pottery, a seemingly important distinction is often drawn between pottery that is "artist-signed" and that which is not. Indeed, this simple distinction may well be a useful one, so long as it does not lead one to make a similar categorical judgment on the artistic merits of the pottery. For example, it is not particularly difficult to find "artist-signed" pots which were produced with but mea-

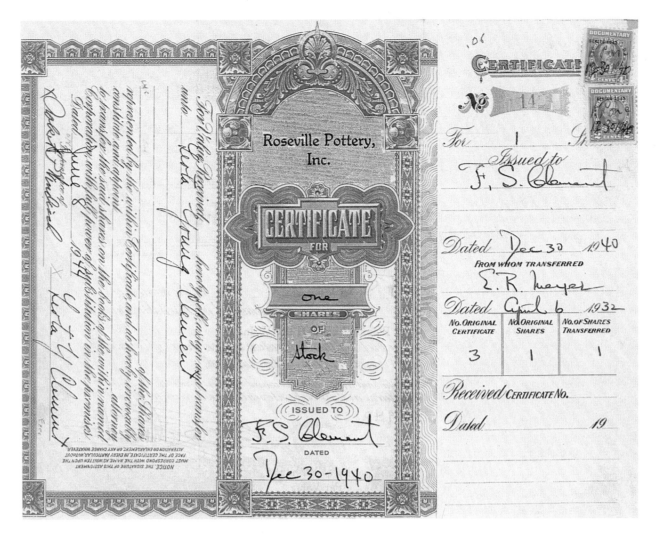

Figure 15B. The reverse side of the stock certificate shown in Figure 15A.

ger artistic standards at best, and it is even easier to find pots totally unsigned which are of great beauty and artistic merit. The owners of various pottery companies in Ohio did little to promote the personal careers of the artisans who created the pottery they sold. While there are many pieces of Peters and Reed Moss Aztec which bear the Ferrell signature, the majority do not. One might guess that Peters and Reed tolerated the practice initially and then discouraged or forbade it; they were interested in promoting their own name and not that of Frank Ferrell. At the Roseville pottery, it was not the practice for the pottery designer to sign the pottery, and in fact the company did not publicize the identity of the creator of its pottery except within the industry itself. Just as with the other potteries, Roseville was interested in advertising its own name, and not that of the artists and artisans who were ultimately responsible for it.

The pottery designed or decorated by Ferrell for Weller, Owens, and Peters and Reed can tell us a lot about the pottery he designed for Roseville. There is a vast artistic depth and enormous variety to the pottery produced by Ferrell before 1918, the year he came to work at Roseville. There are probably also many unsigned pots which he produced for these various potteries, which may one day be identifiable and attributable to him after a comprehensive study of his work has been accomplished. For example, note the tall Weller Aurelian shown in Figure 26, decorated with bunches of grapes and vines. Ferrell was an expert at the art of underglaze painting on pottery, which must have been especially difficult on the dark background of this style of pottery. The difficulty for the artist is that he must paint in colors whose hues will be different after the firing has taken place. Ferrell wrote an article in 1908 for *Keramic Studio*, and McDonald [1989] quotes from it as follows: "Apply color in the same manner as in oil painting. Apply the colors heavily and lay them on smoothly because of burning off in the fire. The grounding and decorating must all be done in the green state while the vase is yet wet." A small pitcher decorated by Ferrell with an egret is shown in Figure 18; this is of the Weller Eocean line and is signed with the letter 'F' only.

Figure 17. A hand-painted diorama of the Roseville Pottery seen from the other side of the Muskingum River. Photo courtesy of the Ohio Historical Society.

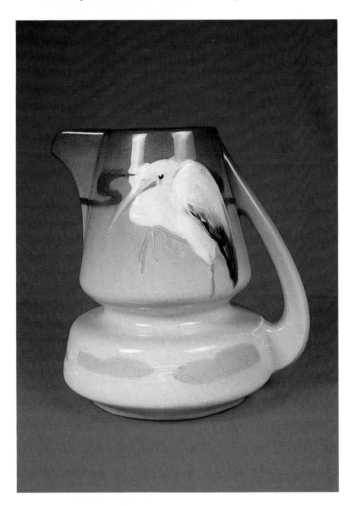

Figure 18. Weller Eocean pitcher decorated by Frank Ferrell with an egret. This piece is signed only with an "F".

Figure 16 [opposite page]. Frank Ferrell shown with a huge piece of Weller, circa 1900. At this time Ferrell was but 22 years old. This vase is now on permanent display at the Zanesville Art Center. Photo courtesy of Mrs. Glen Ridgely and Dick Downey.

Figure 19. A tall Owens vase decorated with Oriental poppies by Frank Ferrell. This vase bears a particularly large and prominent signature, shown in Figure 28.

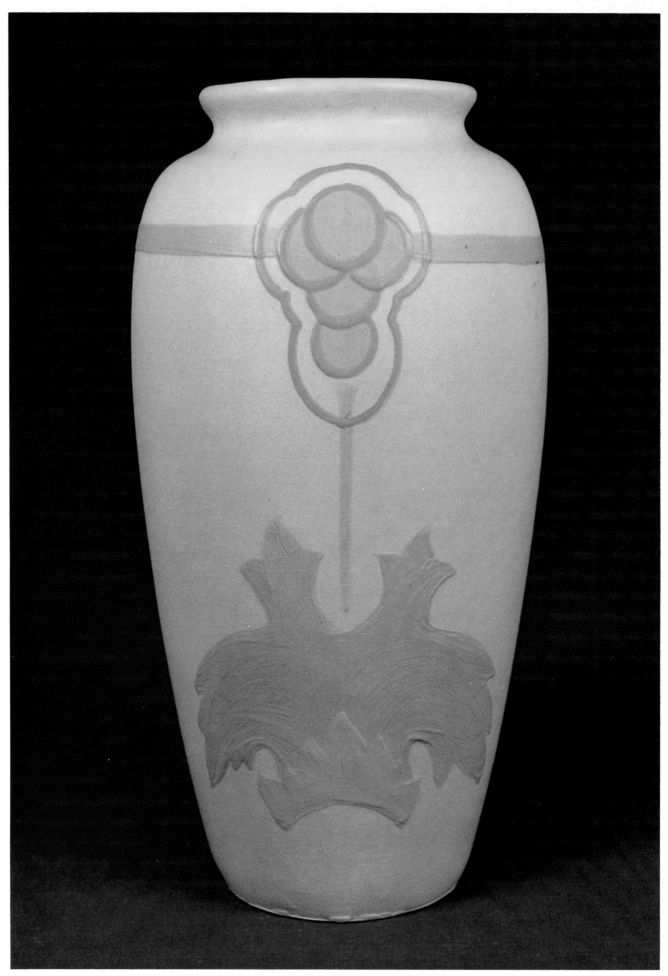

Figure 20. A Weller vase decorated in the Arts and Crafts manner by Frank Ferrell.

Figure 21. A Weller Etched Matte vase by Frank Ferrell.

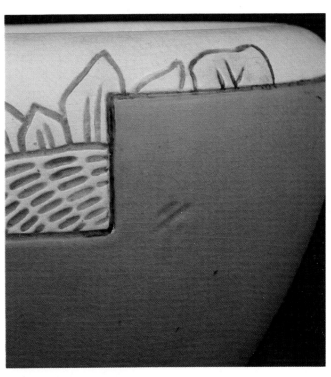

Figure 22. The signature, consisting only of the letter F, for the jardiniere shown in Figure 21.

Figure 23. The Ferrell signature from the Peters and Reed bowl shown in Figure 25.

Figure 24. Peters and Reed Moss Aztec vase decorated with a climbing vine and berries.

Figure 25. Peters and Reed Moss Aztec planter with pinecones designed by Frank Ferrell; signed *Ferrell* in the mold.

Figure 26. A tall Weller Aurelian vase decorated with grapes by Frank Ferrell.

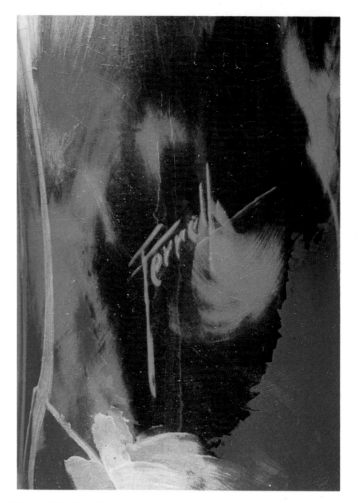

Figure 27. The Ferrell signature for the Weller Aurelian vase shown in Figure 26.

The Weller vase shown in Figure 20 demonstrates rather clearly that Ferrell could easily decorate in the Arts and Crafts style. The decorative motifs appear to be drawn from nature, but they are stylized and abstract. Note that this vase is symmetrical bilaterally and frontally. Such symmetry seems to have been highly prized in Arts and Crafts designs, but it was not particularly typical of Ferrell. This vase bears a beautiful Ferrell signature on the side. More often, Ferrell designs are bilaterally asymmetrical, as the Owens vase shown in Figure 19 demonstrates. This vase, possibly done around 1906 or 1907, uses large oriental poppies to decorate a tall vase in a manner that is very reminiscent of the poppy motifs [in a line of that name] used for Roseville in the late 1930's. This vase bears a huge and beautiful Ferrell signature drawn out in the same violet hue as the petals of the poppies that decorate it.

The Moss Aztec line of pottery which Ferrell designed for Peters and Reed demonstrates designs and techniques of pottery shape creation which are highly relevant to Roseville in some cases. The name Moss Aztec was meant to connote that this pottery was inspired by native American [Mexican] art and that it was a soft, mossy green. This line of utilitarian pottery was made of brick red clay which was then patinated with forest green and rubbed so that the green color remained primarily only in the recesses of the design. The red and green creates a rich contrast, and the design was deeply molded in such a way as to give the pots surprising depth. Often a clear glaze was applied to the inside only of the pot. Examples of Moss Aztec are shown in Figures 24 and 25. Some of these feature flowers which were never used on Roseville, such as the pansy or the black-eyed Susan daisy, but which one could easily imagine might have been developed into lines at Roseville. Some of the pieces of Moss Aztec [probably the earliest ones] are signed by Ferrell in the mold, but most are not. This pottery was probably still in production long after Ferrell had left to design at Roseville.

Photographs of the Ferrell signatures found on these Weller, Owens, and Peters and Reed vases are shown in Figures 22, 23, 27, and 28. The favorite location for the signature seems to have been the lower right side of the vase, where it is not quite visible from

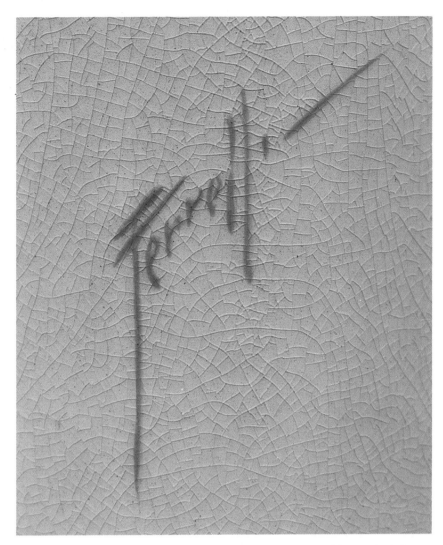

Figure 28. A particularly clear and beautiful Ferrell signature, this from the side of the Owens vase shown in Figure 19. Note the parallel strokes on the 'F', the long parallel 'L's with one distinctly longer than the other one, and the distinctive script 'e' letters. This signature style became the Roseville signature, and is replicated on the bottom of all the pottery produced from the early 1930's onward.

Figures 29A and 29B. Two of many Roseville molded signatures: 29A [above] from a vase in the Bleeding Heart line, circa 1940; 29B [right] from a vase in the Silhouette pattern, circa 1950. There are many different versions of this signature, as it had to be created anew for the master mold of each pot; there are also many interesting slight differences from year to year, but as with any signature, the essential character always remains the same. This was quite literally the signature of Frank Ferrell, since he created it, and in that sense, Roseville pottery is indeed signed by the great artist who conceived it.

the front, but where it is impossible to ignore from the side. The usual Ferrell signature is written on an upward slant, with exaggerated horizontal lines forming part of the F and exaggerated vertical lines forming the final two L's--note these in particular--this one even has a horizontal flourish at the end. The signature is often punctuated with a period and often followed by a horizontal line which makes the entire signature quite prominent and artistic. The Roseville pottery, of course, wanted to promote itself and its own name over and above the name of the man who conceived it and designed it. Therefore, Roseville pottery is not "artist signed" in the same way as other pottery of the period that we are all familiar with. Roseville pottery after about 1932 was marked with the word *Roseville*, either impressed into the pottery or raised above it. There are many versions of the Roseville signature since it

had to be carved into the mold for each piece, and numerous examples are shown here. [Later, the signature was even made as a dealer sign in the Zephyr Lily pattern.] What this demonstrates is that the Roseville signature, which collectors are all so familiar with because it is seen constantly on the bottom of the pottery, that that Roseville signature is, quite literally, the signature of Frank Ferrell himself. Note the overall upward slant, the script "e" and the two long exaggerated l's, one taller than the other. In other words, most Roseville pottery is indeed in a very real sense *though in a different sense*, "artist signed." It bears the signature of the artistic genius who conceived it, and who found a way to put his name clearly upon it. For the greatest part if its existence, the Roseville Pottery and Frank Ferrell were one and the same.

Figure 30. Frank Ferrell and the young Francis 'Hank' Barks, son of Frank Barks, boating on a lake near Zanesville, circa late 1940's. Photo courtesy of William Barks.

Figures 31 [top] and 32 [below] . The Greenwood Cemetery in Zanesville, Ohio: the graves of Charles H. Ferrel [1848-1908]; Elizabeth F. Ferrel [1850-1942]; and Frank L. D. Ferrel [1878-1961]. The graves of Frank Ferrel's sister Edith Earich and her family are located outside the picture further to the right of Frank Ferrel. As one faces these graves, the old route 40 runs along the cemetery on the right and the Interstate 70 along the cemetery on the far left.

About Frank Barks

Frank Hutchinson Barks was born in 1900 in Lancaster, Ohio, and died in 1969 in Zanesville. It is an odd coincidence that Frank Barks began work for the Roseville Pottery around the same time as Ferrell had done, soon after he had graduated from high school, possibly in 1918 or 1919. Frank Barks must have had incredible innate talent as a sculptor, because he was the one chosen by Frank Ferrell to translate his sketches and designs for pottery into actual shapes. There was a very large age difference between Ferrell and Barks. In 1918, the year Ferrell began to work at Roseville, Barks would have been only eighteen, whereas Ferrell was already forty. But by the age of forty, Ferrell had already been working in the field of American art pottery for approximately 25 years. He was by then very experienced in every possible aspect of pottery: he had designed it, decorated it, selected glazes, invented new lines with innovative design, carved his own models, written about it in trade publications, and even acted as a sales representative for it. Ferrell had thus incredibly broad experience in every possible aspect of the art pottery industry, and to some extent he must have acted as a mentor for the young Frank Barks. Frank Barks was also active in the Timber Run Grange, and shared with Frank Ferrell many interests in common, such as the opera and photography.

It is unclear whether Ferrell and Barks began to work together immediately, or after some time, say around 1930. In any event, by the 1930's, the two men worked together in the same office on the third floor of the Roseville factory on Linden Avenue. A unique photograph of Frank Ferrell taken in late 1925 is shown in Figure 10. In all probability this photograph was taken at the Roseville studio shared by Barks and Ferrell. The calendar on the wall clearly shows 1925 as the date. This photograph is interesting because it shows Ferrell around the time he would have been undertaking the design of lines such as Carnelian, Futura, and Imperial, which are certainly among his most beautiful creations.

We are now in a position to better understand exactly how Roseville pottery was actually created. Ferrell himself would originate ideas for lines of pot-

Figure 33. Frank Barks photographed at the college graduation of his son William, in 1956, two years after the Roseville Pottery had closed. Photo courtesy of William Barks.

Figure 34. Frank Barks photographed inside the Roseville Factory, in the studio where he and Ferrell worked side by side. He is seen carving the model for some piece of Roseville pottery; some of his tools lie on a stool in the foreground. We may surmise that this is circa 1944 or 1945. Photographs inside the Roseville factory are quite rare. Photo courtesy of William Barks.

tery, and he would make sketches of what the vases or other objects should look like. Frank Barks then translated Ferrell's sketches into sculpted form and gave them life. In the accompanying photographs, Barks can be seen using his tools to carve the design for a piece, probably of the Freesia line. These photographs were actually taken in the studio of the Roseville Company where both Ferrell and Barks worked together. When Barks had finished carving half of the shape, or in some cases the entire shape, a mold could then be made of it. The forms that Barks created were the "positive" out of which the mold could be made as a "negative." [And additional molds could be made as necessary.] Then, using the mold, or "negative," an almost limitless number of identical examples could be made of each pot. The actual carving tools used by Frank Barks are shown here in Figures 36 and 37. Some of these resemble dental instruments, and many of these tools were probably hand-made themselves.

Many of the molds were created by Vernon Menhorn, whose brother Gene Menhorn also worked at the Roseville factory. Most of the molds were in two sections, but in more complicated or larger designs a four-part mold could be used. A very watery, liquid clay, called slip, was poured into the closed mold and allowed to settle around the sides of the mold. For some items, including large jardinieres, the mold would be put on a jigger, a wheel which would rotate the mold so that the clay would settle evenly around it. After a certain period of time, the mold would be emptied of the liquid slip, leaving a thin layer of clay around the inside of the mold. When the mold was opened, the raw pottery could be removed, and corrected for seam marks and bubbles. The pot was then fired, creating a hard bisque. The bisque was then washed, inspected, and eventually painted and glazed. The pot was then fired again. After the second firing, the pots would be placed on a table to make sure they stood straight, and then often ground on the base to insure that they were perfectly level. Gene Menhorn recalls that someone would check each piece with a tiny hammer to make sure it had no cracks. Inferior examples were discarded, and the others stored on racks for eventual shipment to stores or wholesalers. Gene Menhorn had the job of actually preparing the pottery for shipment. Each piece was individually wrapped in newspaper, then put amid straw in crates for shipment. The pottery left the factory by truck, but it was often shipped to retailers by rail. So much straw was used in this process that a separate shed for straw was constructed next to the factory itself.

When the Roseville Company ceased operations in 1954, this apparently came as a surprise to Frank Barks, and if it was a surprise to him, then we must assume it was also to Frank Ferrell [Interview by the author with Bill Barks, 1996]. Obviously, the true extent of the financial difficulties of the company were not known to its employees, even in this case rather important and long-term ones. Ferrell at that time was already 76 [and still working right up to that point], and so his career as a designer and decorator of American art pottery came then to a sudden end. Frank Barks, on the other hand, needed and was able to find new employment; he did freelance work for the McCoy pottery, with Leslie Cope, and also worked at the Zanesville High School where he did custodial work and helped with their stage productions; he was made an honorary

Figure 35. Frank Barks photographed in his studio carving a model of the Freesia pattern, possibly a wallpocket. Photo courtesy of William Barks.

Thespian there.

The role of Frank Barks in the creation of Roseville pottery has heretofore been totally overlooked in existing works on pottery, and yet his contribution was of great importance. Barks had enormous talent, and his artistry as a sculptor was very important in the overall appearance of the pottery. Since Ferrell and Barks worked so closely and harmoniously together for so many years, and were close personal friends, it is entirely appropriate that their contribution to the design of Roseville pottery be acknowledged here in this book as a truly collaborative work.

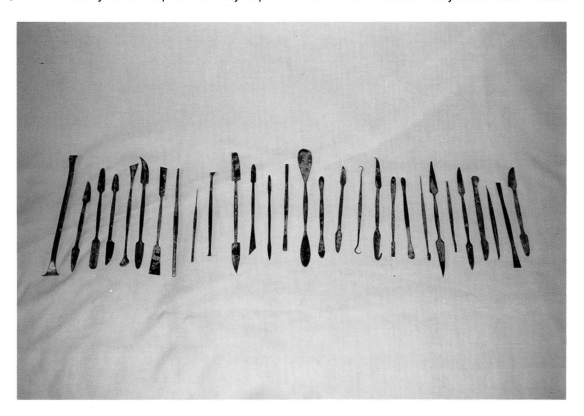

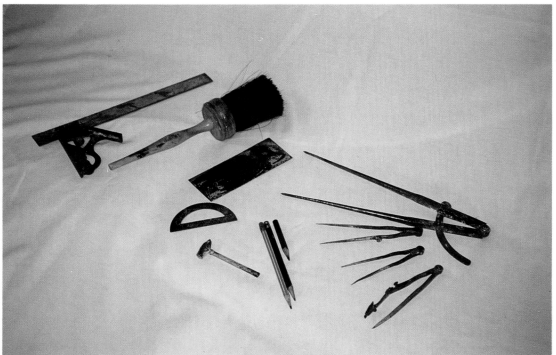

Figure 36 and 37. The original tools used by Frank Barks to carve models of Roseville pottery. Many of them seem to resemble dental instruments, and some of them may have been hand-made. *What a prodigious amount of beautiful art pottery was created with these simple instruments!* One of the models of the Wincraft pattern is shown in this book [Figure 188]. Photo courtesy of Francis Barks.

Ferrell Design Techniques: Shape Telescoping

There were several specific design techniques used by Ferrell to create the vast number of different shapes of pottery produced by Roseville and by the other art pottery enterprises where he worked before coming to Roseville. These techniques were mentioned briefly and schematically in Volume I of the *Collectors' Compendium*. In this volume, one of these techniques, shape telescoping, will be examined in depth; in successive volumes of the *Compendium*, the other remaining techniques will be also discussed in detail. We have coined the term 'shape telescoping' to refer to this design technique because we have never seen it discussed elsewhere. The name itself derives from a pot of the Futura pattern which bears the collectors' nickname 'telescope' for the simple fact that it so strongly resembles one. This technique may not have been recognized and understood at the time as a unique design inspiration, because it was never copied by other art potteries. This is all the more surprising because all of the successful art potteries did in fact competitively produce wares of an unmistakably similar quality and design.

The device called "telescoping" was a favorite Ferrell technique used to give variety, richness, and even a sense of movement to the pottery. *In fact, the telescoping of shape in pottery design practically constitutes a Ferrell signature.* Telescoping was employed often in Futura, and in many other Ferrell patterns, such as Laurel, Falline, Luffa. What "telescoping" means is that part of the vase appears to have been pulled out from inside the other part, with the result that different layers are exposed. In a telescope the parts of its tube are housed inside each other, necessitating that the diameter of each be successively smaller. The shape of a telescoped vessel changes in a quantal manner. Thus, instead of designing a vase which slopes gently and smoothly upward toward its opening as a classical vase does, telescoping allows it to do so dramatically and in a near stepwise fashion. In the Futura pattern, the use of telescoping results in the various step motifs that are common to more than a third of the pieces. An excellent example of this technique is small budvase which in fact has been nicknamed the Telescope Urn, RV#382-7. In other patterns, such as Laurel, the device is used in a more subtle and softer fashion, usually with only one or two "layers," the edges of which are softly rounded. This technique was also used in the styling of handles, such as in the Iris pattern and in Futura. Telescoping imparts movement to a stationary object, precisely because it implies a previous state as well as a possible future one. Telescoping of shape is definitely an important part of the visual impact of a

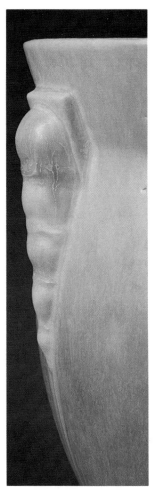

Figure 39. An example of the telescoping of the flower bud motif in Topeo.

Figure 38. The entire shape of this piece of the Clematis line has been created by shape-telescoping; furthermore, its curved shape gives it the feeling of a flower that is opening.

Roseville vase. Roseville pottery would not be the same without it.

According the Roman Jacobson, a Russian linguist who has studied the poetry of many different languages and cultures, the defining common element of all poetry is very simply the repetition or the partial repetition of items. The repetition and especially the partial repetition of sounds, of rhythmic patterns, of words, and even of syntactic patterns and of meanings and ideas is what makes poetry different from prose. This is also an important element in understanding the beauty of music, where our ears respond to a systematic repetition of sounds we call a melody. The use of telescoping to design a vase does the same thing for our eyes that the partial repetition of sounds does for our ears. It rhymes. It creates beauty by providing a visual echo of the shape. It may be Ferrell's single most original design technique. It is one he exploited time and time again—to me it is like a signature, albeit not his only one.

One can find subtle hints of the use of telescoping in Ferrell designs before the Futura and Carnelian lines of 1928, but the major exploitation of this technique of pottery creation begins around 1928 and continues to

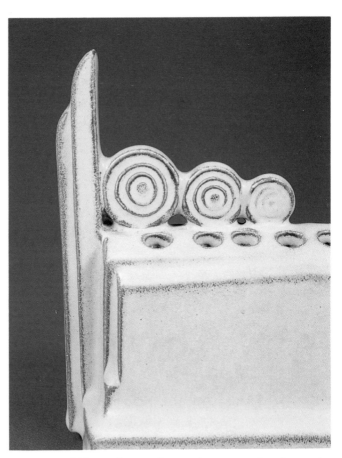

Figure 41. Telescoping can be used to create the shape of a vase, or merely to create a distinctive handle or a decorative motif used to decorate and define the pot. Telescoping was frequently used to create handles on pottery of the late 1930's and 1940's.

Figure 40. The full exploitation of telescoping in the Laurel line, where it is used to create the overall shape and also to design the decorative handles; it conveys movement, dynamism, and excitement to the viewer.

appear robustly thereafter. Shape telescoping was not exploited in the design of the Tuscany pattern, but a mere hint of it does occur in the Cremona pattern of 1927. It could well be that this technique developed literally from its use in Futura and Carnelian. That is, this technique may have been born out of an attempt to produce modernistic forms, but it developed into a full blown general technique for the creation and embellishment of new pottery shapes. In the Futura pattern it was used constantly and with dramatic effect and it can almost be said to define the pattern. The great sense of power and movement that Futura pottery exerts on the viewer derives undoubtedly in no small measure from this technique. The telescoping technique could also be softened by making the number of size increments less, and by rounding the edges of the telescoped parts. This results in a camouflage of the technique, but its artistic effect is not lessened. Softened use of telescoping is found in the Falline pattern and in Wisteria. In many of the later Roseville patterns, telescoping was often used to create stylistically different handles on each pattern, and to underscore the dramatic effect of the handles. The Ixia pattern, for example, is a soft floral pattern, but its telescoped buttress handles are closely related to Futura and help to give the pattern a uniquely Art Deco appearance.

Considerations on Rarity and Prices for Roseville Pottery

The market value of an object is by definition what a typical buyer is willing to pay for it. What price-guides usually attempt to accomplish is to provide the collector with an idea of what price a given object typically is sold for on repeated occasions. Such prices are necessarily "theoretical," in that they are based upon the assumption of a knowledgeable buyer and seller, neither being under undo pressure to sell or buy, respectively. However, in practice, the buyer may know the market better than the seller [or vice versa], and the buyer may be more highly motivated to buy than the seller is to sell [or vice versa]. So any item may actually sell at a price above or below its listing in a price guide. Nevertheless, price guides are very popular with antique collectors; collectors prefer there to be a "book-value" against which they can compare their potential and actual purchases. For many Roseville pieces, it is relatively straightforward to determine a book-value range. These are the more easily found pieces which are sold often enough at antique shows that a price range can be established with relative ease and certitude, at least within a given frame of time. The price ranges of the more frequently sold pieces of pottery can be stated with greater certainty than for the more rarely sold pieces. Other pieces of Roseville are seen and sold so seldom that a valid price range or book value can only be guessed at based upon the value of other pieces whose value is known. In addition, it tends to be somewhat more a "buyers' market" for the more frequently seen pots, and a "sellers' market" for the rarer ones.

Who establishes prices? The *collectors* as a group establish prices; the dealers who sell the items do not. It is interesting that in the perception of many or most collectors, the opposite is thought to be true. In general, antique dealers follow a market, they do not create it, and in many or most cases they have little control over it. However, it is indeed a very popular misconception that the opposite is true—that antique dealers, whether by greed or malice, continually have made the prices of Roseville rise. But it is as silly to assume that antique dealers establish market prices for art pottery as it would be to assume that one's stockbroker or real estate agent determine the selling prices of stocks or houses. They simply do not have this power, regardless of whether they might like to. To the frustration of many collectors, some Roseville lines, such as Futura, Sunflower, and others, have for many years sold at prices substantially above all other lines of Roseville from the "middle-period" era. They have not done so merely because dealers priced them much higher, but rather because the buying public has continually demanded them and been willing to pay for them. Nor does demand appear to have diminished in the presence of rising prices; in fact, the con-tinually rising prices, especially for excellent pieces of many middle-period lines, may have abetted the expanding market.

There have been other price-guides which give some indication of the value of Roseville pottery [e.g., Kovel's *Collectors' Guide to American Art Pottery*, *Collectors' Encyclopedia of Roseville Pottery I and II*, by Huxford and Huxford] but these are not comprehensive treatments. Since much Roseville pottery does not bear any impressed or molded identification marks, some antique dealers occasionally do not recognize what it is. These instances are fortunate for collectors, since they can then sometimes purchase the piece of pottery at a small fraction of its true value. Roseville pottery can be found in the marketplace at prices higher or indeed lower than what is typical or realistic. For both of these situations, the collector can find a price-guide useful. A price-guide can assist the collector to recognize pieces that are advantageously priced for the buyer as well as those which are not. For obvious reasons, the seller is also wise to consult a price guide before deciding to sell.

Occasionally, a piece of Roseville can be found for next to nothing at flea markets or estate sales, but this is becoming less and less possible, and it would be difficult to build a collection of quality and depth in this manner. But however refreshing it is for a collector to find a bargain in this way, the serious collector should realize that a whole collection of quality cannot be acquired by bargain-hunting alone. Many pieces will have to be purchased at fair market value, and the wise collector will hunt for quality first and a bargain second. And it is often true that if the price of a pot is temptingly low, it may have a concealed restoration.

A number of variables bear on the price of pottery, and these variables should be considered in addition to the price. The first and most important of these is the condition of the pot. It is difficult to say what "mint" can really mean when used to refer to pottery that is sixty plus years old, but a reasonable working definition is that it means the same condition as when the pot left the pottery factory which produced it. Most objects which have survived sixty years of existence show some physical sign of that long and perilous journey through time. There may be a small chip on the underside of the pot, and unfortunately very often at the top opening or on any part of the pot that protrudes, such as handles or legs. If the vase has been hit or dropped, it may have a hairline in addition to chips. Because of the rarity and desirability of some Roseville patterns, it is no longer uncommon for a piece to be found in restored condition. Both chips and hairline cracks detract strongly from the market value of the pottery; if the damage is substantial, the value of the piece should be considered approximately half of the price it would otherwise have been. This is especially true for the more easily found pieces. The effect of restorations on the value of pottery is less easy to evaluate, and it depends somewhat on the professional quality of the restoration. Some collectors eschew restored pottery, while others find it tolerable if the piece is rare or desirable enough. The important issue about restoration is that it should be of professional quality and of course the buyer should be aware of it prior to purchasing the pot.

While perfection is desirable, some collectors are unreasonably fanatic about the "mint" nature of their purchases. These individuals will often reject an otherwise excellent piece of pottery simply because of a very minor flat chip on the bottom of the pot. An inconsequential flaw should not prevent a wise collector from acquiring the item, especially on the rarer Roseville pieces. In other words, the collector should bear in mind the inherent rarity of the piece in relation to other pieces of Roseville that are available. Of those pieces that are truly very rare, the collector should consider acquiring them even if they may be in slightly less than absolute mint condition. It is especially unreasonable to expect the jardiniere and pedestal to be without some kind of minor chip, since these were utilitarian items, and they may have seen decades of continuous use. However, in the final analysis, each collector must make his or her own decision about collecting imperfect pieces. It will always be true that pots in excellent condition will command a higher price than those which have sustained damage.

The quality of the mold is another variable which affects the price of the pottery. If the molds were worn through constant use, the impression of the decorative pattern may be weak. This is difficult for a novice collector to evaluate, since it requires one to have seen and compared many different examples of the same line. However, a reputable pottery dealer will often discuss and evaluate this with the collector. Some pieces of Roseville have such an excellent mold that the design appears to have been freshly carved into the pottery with a penknife, as for example the bamboo leaves on the Futura jardiniere and pedestal. On pieces with poor mold, one discerns the design primarily through the painting. Pots with poor mold can more easily be found in patterns produced in the early 1940's and especially in the Pinecone pattern since production demands caused the molds to be overused.

An additional variable for the collector to consider is the quality of the color and glaze. If the pot is of the type to have had a crystalline matte glaze, the question to be asked concerns the richness of the glaze. If there is severe crazing of the glaze, this may also be considered to negatively effect the selling price. Here also, crazing is not a particularly common flaw in some lines, such as Futura, Blackberry, or Cremona,

whereas it is common in other patterns, such as Apple Blossom or Ming Tree.

The colors may also be subject to variation, and this variation may affect price. For example, in the Futura line there are three high-glaze pots which are decorated in pink and greenish gray. These colors may vary between dull gray and light pink to deep pink and deep green. In fact, the predominance of gray in this color pattern is so common that some collectors mistakenly refer to the colors as pink and gray. The brilliance of the colors is another difficult factor for the collector to evaluate, and here again it would be wise to discuss this question with the seller or other collectors.

Roseville pots with experimental glaze or color treatment are not numerous, but their value would be typically at least double the value of the standard counterpart. Occasionally a pot will turn up with exceptionally poor application of color, and this of course should not be mistaken as a color variation.

The Japanese are known to have made imitations of Roseville pottery during the 1920's and 1930's. It is well known that Japanese imitations of the Montacello and Cherry Blossom pattern exist. Sometimes they copied Roseville as porcelain. For example, there exists a Noritake budvase in the exactly the same shape as one of Ferrell's Dogwood II designs. The Japanese also copied Futura, although the extent to which they did so is difficult to determine. It is most likely that only certain pieces of the line were copied. Vase #197-6 [the Half Egg] is known to exist in the form of a Japanese copy, and presumably there were others imitated as well. In comparison with the genuine Futura or Montacello, the Japanese imitations are woefully easy to recognize. The overall quality of the pot is inferior, it is lighter in weight and the colors are garish and crudely applied. In the case of the Japanese imitation of Futura #197-6, the green color is applied at the top in such a way as to resemble a green stripe—nothing at all like the subtle coloring of the

---

Important Factors to consider in evalutating Roseville Pottery:

Color
Mold
Rarity
Condition
Price

genuine pot. Fortunately, these pieces are not common. Their value should be considered negligible. In addition to these 'old' reproductions, new ones are now being made, apparently in China or Taiwan. The quality of these 1990's repros is so poor as to place them beneath contempt, and even a beginning collector could recognize them for what they are: cheap imitations. Imitation, when done so poorly, is never flattering to the original.

Roseville pots also differ as to their relative desirability. The more desirable the pot, the more numerous are the collectors who may want to purchase it. For example, aside from rarity, the console bowls are not typically among the most desirable pieces in the minds of most collectors. On the other hand, the tall ten, twelve, and fifteen-inch vases are constantly in demand by collectors who actually may not wish to collect more than several pieces of any one pattern. Many wallpockets are not extremely rare, but they seem to be in constant demand. In general, Futura pieces which exhibit three-dimensional asymmetry and polylinearity have always been in high demand [and very short supply]. Large vases and jardinieres and pedestals in most all Roseville patterns are always in short supply and high demand.

How accurate are the price guides shown in this book? That depends; *caveat lector*. A "price-guide" for stocks and bonds is published every day in major newspapers. It is published daily at great expense because the prices of stocks change from day to day. The prices of antique pottery also change, and sometimes to an astonishing degree, in a rather short time. But in the antique marketplace, we cannot afford the luxury of price guides which are updated on a daily, weekly, or monthly basis, even though there may be changes in prices over several months, and certainly over several years. Therefore, caution in using price guides for antiques is always warranted. Because antiques represent a totally fixed supply, any change in buyer demand can cause a dramatic surge in price, because the supply of them cannot also compensate by increasing.

The prices given in this book are for pots in fine, mint condition, with excellent mold, color, and glaze. The effect of a small underbase chip typically reduces price by 25%, depending on the size and location of the chip. Larger chips [or restorations to them] may reduce the value of the pot by 50% or even more. The prices are not estimates of what price the item should sell for, but ranges within which the piece actually does sell for. That is, these price ranges reflect fair market value. *Fair market value can be defined as the most probable price at which a item would sell for between a willing seller and a willing buyer, when neither are under unusual pressure to sell or to buy, and when both buyer and seller have a reasonable knowledge of the appropriate market.*

The current prices for those Roseville lines seen in *Volume I* and *Volume II* of the *Collectors' Compendium of Roseville Pottery* are to be found in the accompanying booklet.

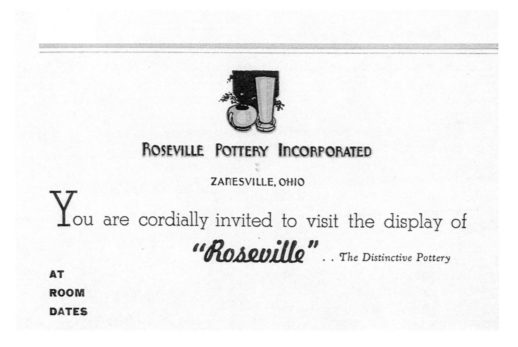

Figure 42. A promotional trade card used by the Roseville Company, probably circa late 1930's. Salesmen could use this to publicize the wholesale display of new lines at hotels or merchandise markets. The two pots shown appear to be of Orian on the left and Moderne on the right. The Roseville style *was* distinctive....then, just as it is now.

BANEDA

The name 'Roseville' itself refers to the little town south of Zanesville where the pottery originated, although roses themselves figured seldom in the decoration of Roseville pottery. The names for individual pottery lines were often fancifully made up, sometimes partially of references to people who worked at the pottery, sometimes partially of meaningless syllables which combined to produce a pleasant sounding word. For example, Russco is a reference to Russell Young who became president of the Roseville pottery after the death of George Young. Falline may simply have been 'fall' + 'line,' but when combined the whole is pronounced differently than the parts. Oddly, the company did not use the names of the lines as a marketing strategy in their ads except in the case of Futura. The name Baneda resists clear linguistic analysis, but a good guess is that is from 'Band' [of flowers] + 'needs.' In the handwritten notes of George Krause, it is spelled Baneeda. This may imply that Ferrell first designed the shapes of the Baneda line before adding the band of flowers which so distinctively characterizes the entire line. The Baneda line was probably produced beginning in 1932 and for some years after. The company stockbook page has the date 1933 written on one of the vases.

The floral decoration for the Baneda line consists of a botanical motif which may correspond realistically to nature or which instead may simply be the fanciful creation of Frank Ferrell. However, if it is a realistic representation of some flora, it must certainly be one rare enough that most people do not recognize it and are unable to name it. It consists of white flowers with five pointed petals which impart to the flower a star-shape appearance; these flowers are accompanied by "berries" or fruit which in every respect resemble small pumpkins, and irregular leaves with points, not unlike holly leaves. Whatever fruit is being depicted here, it would definitely seem to have lobes, and the fact is that many collectors refer to them as pumpkins. Whatever this unusual plant represents, its first appearance was not on the Baneda line of pottery, but rather on the Panel line. However, the plant in question has different flowers in the Panel line [the petals are not as long or as pointed], and possibly different leaves as well. The complex stems and branches also are a part of the artistic depiction of this plant.

The design of Baneda in all cases uses a band which occupies typically approximately one-fourth to one-third of the entire height of the pot. The proportion of the pot occupied by the decorative band is least for the very tall ones and greater for the low pieces such as bowls. The band is always placed near the top of the piece, except in the case of candlesticks,

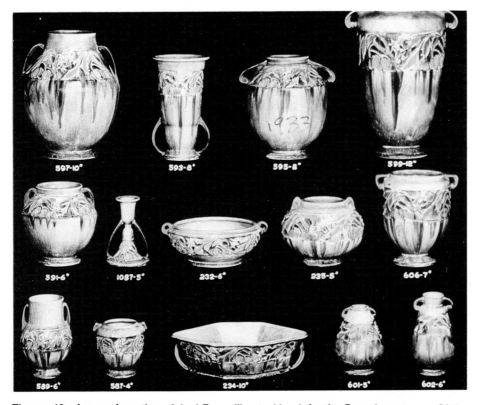

Figure 43. A page from the original Roseville stockbook for the Baneda pattern. Of the three pages for this pattern, one is all of 'green' Baneda, one all of the 'pink', while the third page showing the jardinieres and pedestals features pots of both colors. Photo courtesy of the Ohio Historical Society.

Figure 44. A page from the original Roseville stockbook for the Baneda pattern. Baneda pots vary enormously in relative rarity, as do those of the Futura pattern; some are very rare in one of the two color patterns, but not so in the other color. Photo courtesy of the Ohio Historical Society.

Figure 45. A page from the original Roseville stockbook for the Baneda pattern. This page shows the many jardinieres; a jardiniere and pedestal in the Baneda line is a proud achievement for any collector. Photo courtesy of the Ohio Historical Society.

where it encircles the base. This band of flowers not only decorates the pottery, but it gives the pots great visual depth, since Ferrell used here the underlayer design technique [see Volume I, p. 19] in which the flowers and leaves are placed against a background of vertical striations which makes them stand out against it.

The Baneda line also uses the elegant construction of handles on all of the pots except for one pair of candlesticks. The handles for Baneda are nonfunctional for the most part: they were meant to decorate the pot. In some cases they are placed at the bottom of the vase, and in other cases they are so small that one could hardly hold the vase by them. The handles have the same motif in all cases: curvilinear with a small round part where the handle attaches to the vase. The handles may bend upward or downward. In only one case, that of vase #593-8, is the decorative device called telescoping used.

The Baneda pattern was produced in two separate color pattern combinations, each dramatically different from the other. They are referred to

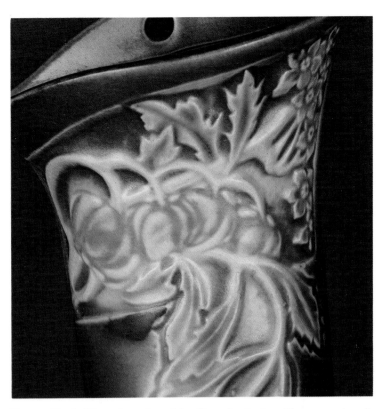

Figure 46. A different version of the Baneda plant motif was used earlier, in the Panel line, as seen on this wallpocket. But note that the leaves and the flowers are different; there are four [rather than three] clusters of berries, and they are violet rather than orange.

Figure 47. The elements of the Baneda design: star-form flowers, orange pumpkin-like berries, and leaves. The design is carved over an incised pattern of vertical lines--*a design underlayer*--which enhances its depth.

by collectors as "green Baneda" and "pink Baneda." The first is deep green, with the flowers in cream and the fruit in orange. In addition, blue color was used on the background in such a way that it is made to drip downward and blends with the deep green of the pot. Thus, the "green" Baneda uses <u>four</u> different colors. The colors of the pot give an overall appearance of richness and vibrancy. Most collectors of green Baneda seek out examples which have very prominent blue glaze streaks coming down from the band of flowers. It is possible to locate examples of green Baneda which have very little of this glaze-dripping effect. In some pieces of the green Baneda, there is an additional fifth color, sandy tan, used to create a blush on one side of the vase. For example, vase #599-12 [as well as some others] have a definite prominent area of tan on one side of the vase. On other pieces, for whatever reasons, this blush is less prominent or missing altogether. This tan color would appear to actually be the color of the clay pot itself.

Figure 48. The unglazed base of model 596 [typically marked with orange/red crayon], with a small foil label.

Figure 49. The fully glazed base of model 597 [also marked with orange/red crayon], with a large size foil label.

In contrast, the pink Baneda uses a bright background of mottled pink, not totally dissimilar from the glaze and color of the Tuscany line, but with greater color intensity. The colors of the band of flowers and leaves are the same: bright orange berries, cream flowers, green leaves, and a blue background. In most pieces of the pink Baneda, there is no dripping of the glaze downward from the flower band. Collectors of today prefer that there be no glaze dripping on the pink Baneda, whereas they demand it on the green color pattern. [Pieces of pink Baneda with strong glaze drips are generally eschewed by collectors.] In the catalogue pages for this pattern, one can clearly see that the green vases and pots shown all have prominent blue dripping effects, whereas all the examples of the pink colored pots are totally devoid of it. The overall impression of pink Baneda in the households of the 1930's must have been really dramatic, since these interiors were often devoid of bright color.

There is a third color combination for Baneda, but it is so rare that its status is more nearly like that of a trial glaze piece. This we could call "blue Baneda," an example of which is shown in Figures 60 and 71. Here, the background color is definitely blue, and the drips are definitely green. Because the two main color patterns for this line are each so different from the other, most collectors collect one to the exclusion of the other. It is interesting that the bottom surfaces of Baneda are [most typically, but not always] unglazed in green, but glazed in pink.

Overall, Baneda is one of the most desirable of the Roseville middle-period patterns. The three catalogue pages for Baneda are shown in Figures 43, 44, and 45. One page illustrates all pieces in green, one

shows them all in pink, and one shows a few of both. Baneda pots differ dramatically in rarity one from the other, and the rarity can be notably different in a few cases for the pink as opposed to the green pattern. For example, vase #604-7 is not particularly rare in the pink color, but it is extremely rare in green. The jardinieres and pedestals are rare in both colors. The wallpocket is quite scarce in green, but it is still rarer in pink. All of these differences are reflected in the price guide which accompanies this book. In the following listing of mold numbers and their shapes, note the skipped mold numbers 236, as well as 607, 608, and 609. A total of 36 different shapes for the Baneda pattern are listed here:

Figure 50. The unglazed base of model 593 with the earlier black paper label.

BANEDA

RV Mold #	Type	RV Mold #	Type
#15-2.5	Flower frog	#600-15	Floor vase
#15-3.5	Flower frog	#601-5	Budvase
		#602-6	Budvase
#232-6	Console bowl	#603-4	Vase
#233-8	Console bowl	#604-7	Vase
#234-10	Console bowl	#605-6	Vase
#235-5	Rose bowl	#606-7	Vase
#237-12	Console bowl		
		#610-7	Vase
#587-4	Bowl vase		
#588-6	Budvase	#626-4	Jardiniere
#589-6	Vase	#626-5	Jardiniere
#590-7	Budvase	#626-6	Jardiniere
#591-6	Vase	#626-7	Jardiniere
#592-7	Vase	#626-8	Jardiniere and Pedestal
#593-8	Vase	#626-9	Jardiniere
#594-9	Vase	#626-10	Jardiniere and Pedestal
#595-8	Vase		
#596-9	Vase	#1087-5	Candleholders [pair]
#597-10	Vase	#1088-4	Candleholders [pair]
#598-12	Vase		
#599-12	Vase	#1269	Wallpocket

Figure 51. Baneda model #601-5, in green.

Figure 52. Baneda model #587-4, in green, the smallest piece in the entire line.

Figure 53. A Baneda lampbase, shown here without the lamp parts.

Figure 54. A rosebowl with very abbreviated handles, Baneda model #235-5.

Figure 55. A ball-form vase, Baneda model #591-6, which is about as wide as it is tall.

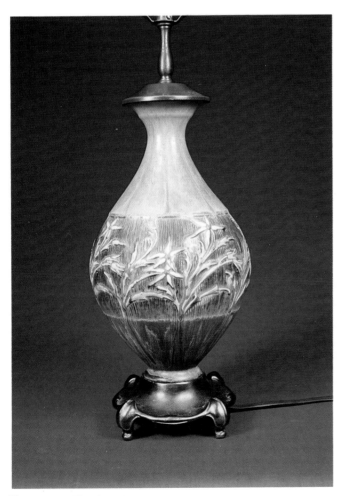

Figure 56. The lampbase seen on the opposite page, with its complete assembly; the pottery bears a black paper label and the notation F11. Note the "Baneda" plant motif, here in a somewhat different form, and without its usual fruit.

Figure 57. The elusive Baneda wallpocket, model #1269.

Figure 58. Baneda model #592-7 in green.

Figure 59. Baneda model #596-9 in green.

Figure 60. Baneda model #589-6 in "blue"; its more common counterpart is seen in Fig. 61. Trial glazes often occur on this vase model.

Figure 61. Baneda model #589-6 in green; Baneda colors were probably derived from the Earlam and Artcraft lines.

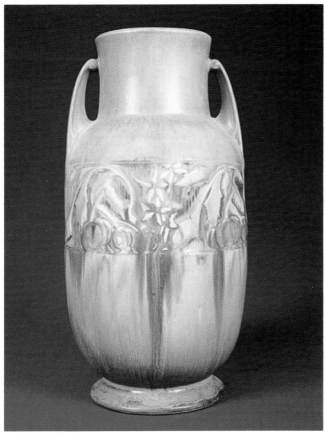

Figure 62. Baneda model #594-9 in green.

Figure 63. Baneda model #595-8 in green.

Figure 64. A Baneda budvase, model #588-6, in green.

Figure 65. Baneda model #590-7 in green.

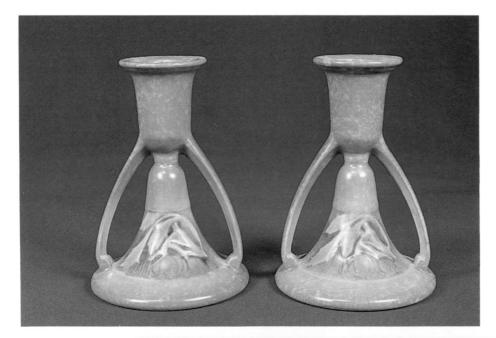

Figure 66. Baneda pink candlesticks, model #1087-5.

Figure 67. Baneda console bowl, model #232-6 in pink.

Figure 68. Baneda urn model #591-6 in pink. Note the cleanness of the colors and the lack of any dripping effects---a clear contrast with the esthetics of the green color pattern. This model is also exceptional in that there are four clusters of berries rather than the usual three.

Figure 69. Baneda model #588-6 in pink.

Figure 70. Baneda model #604-7 in pink; note the unusual lack of blue around the base.

Figure 71. Baneda console bowl model #232-6 in blue/green; this would be called an example of "blue" Baneda.

Figure 72. A pair of green Baneda candlesticks with elegant looped handles, model #1087-5.

Figure 73. A green Baneda console bowl, model #233-8.

Figure 74. A pair of green Baneda candlesticks with hexagonal bases, model #1088-4; these were undoubtedly meant to accompany the huge hexagonal console bowl, model #237-12.

Figure 75. A green Baneda console bowl, model #234-10; this bowl has six sides to it, but it is oblong in shape.

Figure 76. An extremely large hexagonal console bowl, model #237-12.

Figure 77. An example of the Baneda jardineres, in green, model #626-6.

Figure 78. A superb pair of green Baneda jardinieres and pedestals, #626-8 and #626-10. Collection of Curt Rustand.

Figure 79 [right]. A pink Baneda jardiniere and pedestal, model #626-10. Collection of Curt Rustand.

Figure 80. Baneda model #610-7 in green; this "ice-bucket" shape is quite uncommon, especially in green.

Figure 81. Baneda model #606-7 in green.

Figure 82. The green Baneda Jardiniere and Pedestal, #626-10.

Figure 84. Baneda model #603-4 in green.

Figure 83. Baneda model #626-4 in green, the smallest among seven jardinieres; because they are different sizes of the same design, they will all tend to look the same when photographed individually.

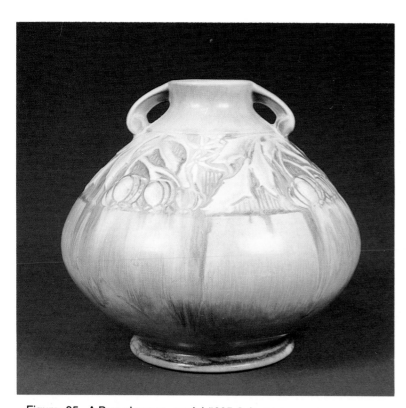

Figure 85. A Baneda vase, model #605-6, in green.

Figure 86. Baneda model #602-6 in green.

Figure 87. Green Baneda vase model #604-7; this model is very difficult to find in green.

Figure 88. Green Baneda vase, model #593-8, the only clear example of the use of shape telescoping in the entire line.

Figure 89. The green Baneda vase, model #597-10.

Figure 90. Green Baneda vase #599-12, an imposing piece which beautifully exemplifies the line.

Figure 91. Green Baneda vase #598-12, with elegant inverted handles.

Figure 92. The green Baneda floor vase #600-15; the glaze and color effects are always different on each of these.

CREMONA

The Cremona line of pottery, a relatively narrow line, was produced in the late 1920's. While the date of 1927 has been given for this line [since that is when ads for it appear in magazines], the Roseville company stockbook page has the dates 1924-1928 penciled in on one of the vases [by whom we do not know]. The name itself is interesting and somewhat of a puzzle. It may simply have been a euphonious sequence of syllables, or possibly an obscure reference to a play of Shakespeare. But oddly, Cremo itself was a Roseville line which had appeared earlier. There are two known different color patterns for this line, and they both have cream-colored overglaze which tends to soften the depiction of the botanical motifs on the pottery and give it a very impressionistic rather than realistic quality. What makes Cremona so different from other Roseville lines of pottery is that the botanical motifs used to decorate it are quite diverse, and they are not carried out with the same degree of realism as in later patterns, such as, for example, Pinecone.

One color pattern used for this line depicts the botanical motifs in light blue and medium green on a light green background. The other color pattern uses the same colors to decorate the flowers and leaves, but against a pink background. Those pots decorated on the pink background appear to have a light green overglaze also. Many different flora are used in this

pattern, and most of them would appear to be wildflowers. The entire line seems to have a very Arts and Crafts spirit to it, possibly because the flowers and leaves tend to be placed on the pots in a symmetrical manner, as opposed to the more typical Ferrell preference for placing the flowers asymmetrically on vases, as in the Wisteria pattern and most others. In addition, the shapes of the Cremona line are also all symmetrical in the bilateral and frontal planes of reference.

Since Cremona is one of the very early lines designed by Ferrell at the Roseville pottery, many of his most characteristic design techniques are absent or seen only in incipient form. However, this line possibly contains one of the very first examples of the use of telescoping in pottery design, a technique that was later to be used by Ferrell extensively to create hundreds of new pottery shapes. There is some use of handles in this line, and this use foreshadows what would become a much more extensive exploitation of handles as decorative devices on pottery. The handles are used in Cremona not in a manner so as to define the line, but in a few cases to embellish and continue the form of the pot. They tend not to be functional but rather decorative, and they have no resemblance to the botanical motifs used on the pots as decoration.

The bottom surfaces of Cremona pots are glazed, but there is no molded Roseville mark. Some pieces retain a paper sticker. There is no wallpocket

Figure. 93. The Roseville catalogue page for the Cremona pattern. The photograph was hand-colored, seemingly all shown in the green color line. Photo courtesy of the Ohio Historical Society.

in this pattern, nor sizable jardinieres. As of this writing, the prices for Cremona are far below that of other Roseville lines comparable to it. It is almost as if collectors have not discovered it. But Cremona is very beautiful, and collectors will indeed awaken to it. The line consists of the following 20 different shapes:

RV Mold #	Type
#72-4	Fan budvase
#73-5	Fan budvase
#74-6	Fan budvase
#75	Flower frog
#176-6	Bowl
#177-8	Console bowl
#178-8	Console bowl
#351-4	Vase
#352-5	Vase
#353-5	Bowl/vase
#354-7	Vase
#355-8	Vase
#356-8	Vase
#357-8	Vase
#358-10	Vase
#359-10	Vase
#360-10	Vase
#361-12	Vase
#362-12	Vase
#1068-4	Candleholders [pair]

Figure 94. Cremona model #356-8 in green, a trumpet-form vase.

Figure 95. Cremona miniature fan vase, model #73-5, in green.

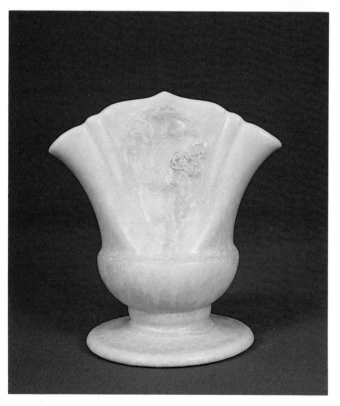

Figure 96. Cremona model #73-5 in pink.

Figure 97. Cremona model #74-6 in green.

Figure 98. Cremona model #353-5 in green.

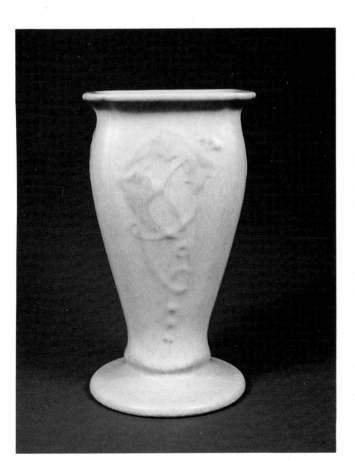

Figure 99. Cremona vase, model #354-7, in green.

Figure 100. Cremona vase, model #352-5, in green.

Figure 101. A green Cremona console bowl, model #178-8, with the frog #75.

Figure 102. A square Cremona console bowl, model #177-8.

Figure 103. The Cremona candlesticks, model #1068-4, in green.

Figure 104. A green Cremona bowl, model #176-6.

Figure 105. Green Cremona vase, model #351-4.

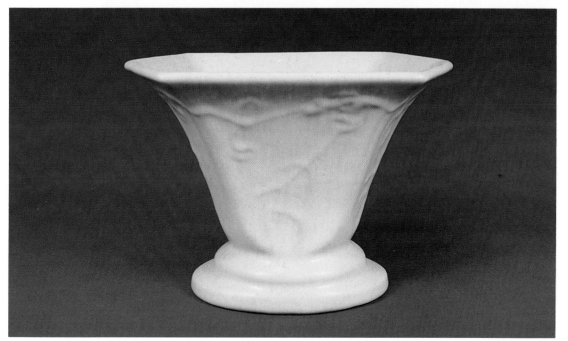

Figure 106. A green Cremona fan vase, model #72-4.

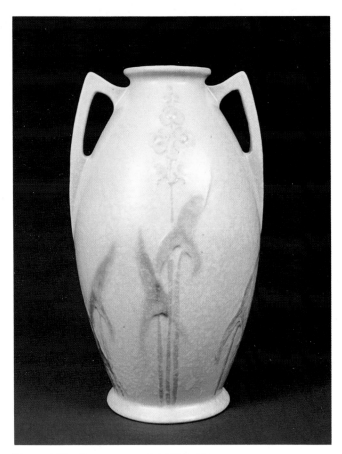

Figure 107. Cremona model #359-10 in green.

Figure 108. Cremona model #355-8 in green.

Figure 109. Cremona vase, model #360-10, in green.

Figure 110. Cremona vase, model #357-8, in green.

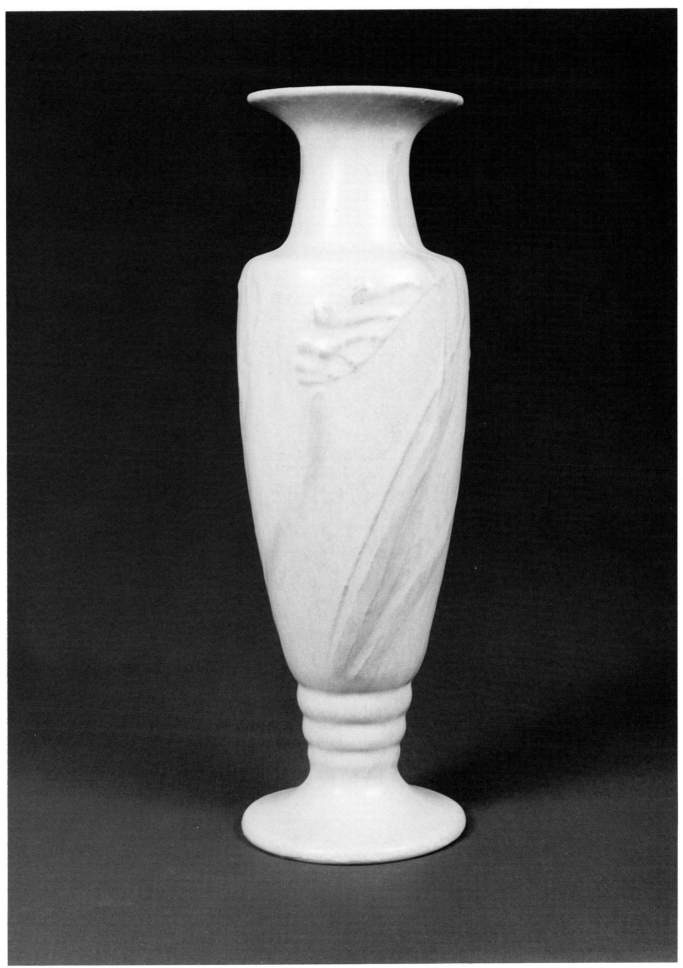

Figure 111. Green Cremona vase #361-12.

Figure 112. Pink Cremona vase, model #358-10.

Figure 113. Pink Cremona vase, model #362-12.

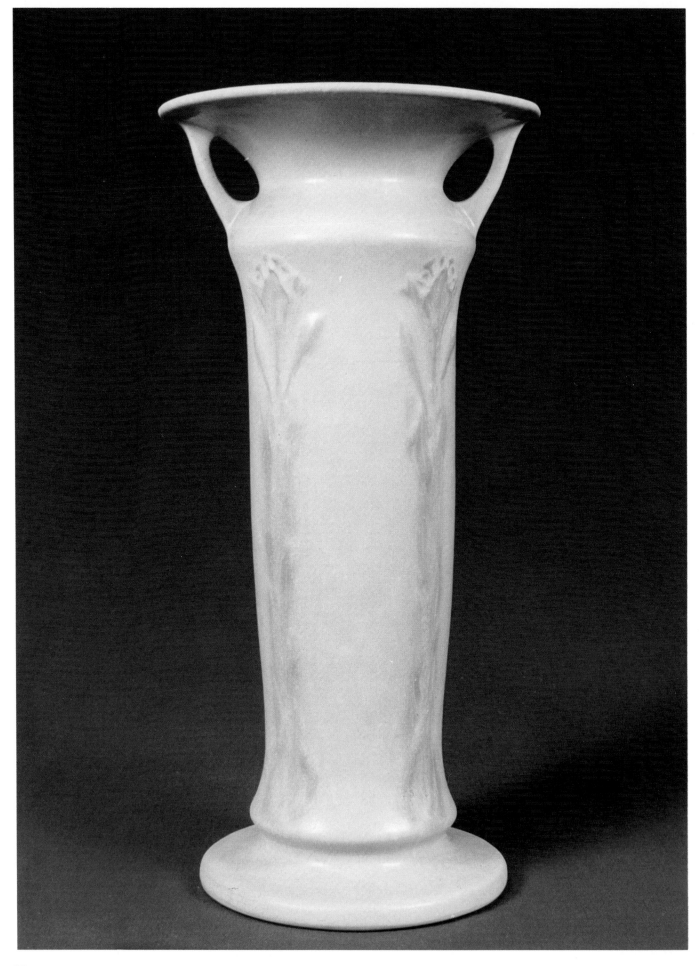

Figure 114. Green Cremona vase, model #362-12.

FERELLA

The Ferella pattern was of course named after its creator, Frank Ferrell; the spelling was altered to correspond more naturally to how the new name was to be pronounced. According to the Schneider interview with Ferrell, the Roseville Company wanted to call the new line simply "Ferrell," but the designer would not permit it, whereas he agreed to the modified name Ferella. Ferella is one of the most beautiful and elegant lines of the Roseville "middle" period, but yet there are many ways in which it is atypical of most other Roseville. First, it is symmetrical in two of three possible planes of reference: it is frontally and mid-sagittally symmetrical. Such symmetry is typical of much Arts and Crafts pottery but it is atypical of most of Ferrell-designed Roseville pottery. Second, it uses no floral decoration other than a very abstract grouping of "buds." Thirdly, it uses cut-out designs in the pottery. However, it is a characteristic Ferrell design in that it uses telescoping quite often to create new shapes, it uses the contrasting colors typical of many Art Deco designs, and it features rich, vibrant color and lustrous glaze which invariably hold the viewer's eyes once they have fallen upon it. The glaze is enriched considerably by the application of white overglaze apparently splashed upon the pottery so that it appears in spots. This line of pottery superbly dem-onstrates Ferrell's versatility and creativity as a designer. Part of the esthetic appeal of this pottery is that the cut-out portions at the top and the bottom create the illusion of lightness and airiness, and even of mystery—since the eye assumes the bottom of a pot should be solid and enclosed, while Ferella pots are not.

The decoration of Ferella consists of elaborate cut-outs on both the base and top of the vase, alternated with a plant-like motif. What is this motif? The motif is abstract and stylized enough that it cannot be said to resemble any particular flower, but it appears as a standing symmetrical band of buds [in some cases nine, and in some cases seven of them or even as few as five]. We may presume that the cut-out portions of the design were created by cutting into the greenware before firing into bisque, and so there may somewhere exist examples without the cut-out portions, though we have never seen any. Ferella was produced in a brown and green color combination, and also in red and green. The brown/green decoration actually appears to have four colors, since the paint was wiped away from the buds so that they appear as yellow, and the bottom of the vase uses a second dark brown, almost black. Likewise, the red/green Ferella appears for the same reason to have a third or fourth

Figure. 115. The original catalogue page from the Roseville stockbook for the Ferella line. Photo courtesy of the Ohio Historical Society.

color, pink on the bud stems and yellow on the buds. The bottom surfaces of Ferella pots are unglazed, and bear no Roseville signature; small black paper labels are common on many pieces.

There is a Ferella lamp base, similar to the vase model #507-9, which was produced in many colors, including all green, all blue, and golden tan [and possibly other colors]. It would appear that the red variety of Ferella is the most artistically successful, and that is decidedly the variety that is in the greatest demand today. There are numerous trial color varieties of Ferella extant, and they are often of stunning beauty. Some of them are shown in this book. It was often the practice to transfer the colors and glazes developed in one line of pottery onto another line. Thus, two of the trial glazed pots shown here use the colors of Futura and of Topeo, and there probably would exist other trial glaze pieces with colors reminiscent of other pre-Ferella lines such as Tuscany or Cremona or Earlam. In other words, both colors and glazes that were developed in one line were tried and often exploited in other lines. Thus, the colors used in green Baneda were developed from those used in Artcraft and Earlam, the bright emerald green used in Futura derives from Savona, and so forth. What is particularly interesting about the trial color and glaze examples in the Ferella line is that they used an elaborate blank which was later simplified for the standard production. On the color-trial models, the array of buds is much more larger, with the result that there are 17 and 19 buds in a bunch. Whereas most pieces of Roseville pottery in good condition will "ring" when tapped lightly with the finger, Ferella—because of its cut-outs at the top of each piece—will not in most cases. Many of the Ferella shapes are now quite scarce, especially those which can easily fall over, such as #501-6. One of the most popular models may have been #497-4, a budvase with flared handles.

The known Ferella shapes consist of the following:

RV Mold #	Type
#15-2.5	Frog, for #211
#15-3.5	Frog, for #212
#87-8	Console bowl /attached frog
#210-4	Bowl
#211-8	Round bowl
#212-12-7	Oblong bowl
#497-4	Budvase
#498-4	Small vase
#499-6	Vase
#500-5	Vase
#501-6	Vase
#502-6	Vase
#503-5	Vase
#504-5.5	Vase
#505-6	Vase
#506-8	Vase
#506-8	Vase, trial shape
#507-9	Vase [Lamp base]
#508-8	Vase
#509-8	Vase
#510-9	Vase
#511-10	Vase
#620-5	Flower pot/attached dish
#1078-4	Candlesticks, pair
#1266-6.5	Wallpocket

Figure 116. This is a trial shape and color in the Imperial II line, model #585-4. In the Imperial II line it was produced in a pink and green color, but possibly only on a trial basis. The shape has the characteristic bands that are the hallmark of Imperial II. The color differs from Ferella in that the red is brighter, and the white spattered overglaze color was applied rather abundantly, and thus it lacks the subtlety of this technique as it was actually used in Ferella. This spatter technique was also used much earlier, for example, in Cremona.

Figure 117. An unusual Ferella console bowl with an attached frog, model #87-8, in red. This item was probably popular with consumers of the 1920's.

Figure 118. An oblong console bowl, #212-12-7, in red. This is a very large piece of pottery and it has a particularly elegant and pleasing shape.

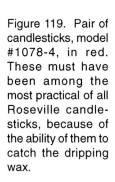

Figure 119. Pair of candlesticks, model #1078-4, in red. These must have been among the most practical of all Roseville candlesticks, because of the ability of them to catch the dripping wax.

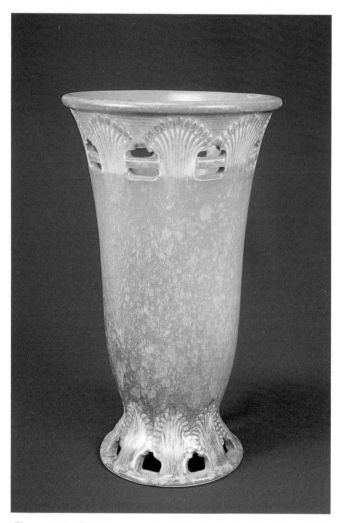

Figure 120. Ferella model #506-8, with trial colors that derive primarily from Topeo. The buds are painted in deep yellow. Collection of Greg Koster.

Figure 121. Ferella model #506-8, with trial colors that derive primarily from Futura. The buds are painted in Futura/Savona green. Collection of Gordon Hoppe.

Figure 122. Ferella miniature or cabinet vase, model #498-4, in brown.

Figure 123. Ferella vase #503-5, with a wide decorative border, in brown.

Figure 124 [top]. Ferella console bowl #211-8 in red. Figure 125. [immediately above] Flower Frog #15-3.5 in red.

Figure 126. The Ferella walpocket, #1266-6.5, in red.

Figure 127. Red Ferella budvase #502-6.

Figure 128. A red Ferella vase, model #508-8. Note its extremely narrow base.

Figure 129. Red Ferella bowl #210-4.

Figure 130. A bowl for flowers, Ferella #505-6, in red.

Figure 131. A red Ferella budvase with decorative handles, model #497-4

Figure 132. A red Ferella flower pot and its attached underplate, #620-5.

Figure 133. A red Ferella vase, #510-9, whose expansive handles gracefully complete its ovoid shape.

Figure 134. Red Ferella vase, #507-9.

Figure 135. Red Ferella vase #500-5.

Figure 136. Red Ferella ball-shaped vase #509-8.

Figure 137. A red Ferella vase, #504-5.5. It telescopes downward and the base is so narrow it appears almost upside down.

Figure 138. Red Ferella budvase #499-6, shown here larger than its actual size.

Figure 139. Ferella vase #501-6, in red, shown larger than its actual size.

Figure 140. Red Ferella vase #511-10, the largest and possibly the most beautiful vase in the line.

Figure 141. Brown Ferella vase #506-8, the standard model; note how the cut-out parts differ from the trial shape in Figure 142.

Figure 142. Ferella vase #506-8, a trial shape and in trial colors which are quite similar to the standard.

LAUREL

The Laurel pattern is a very narrow pattern, but it is keenly appreciated by collectors of Roseville pottery designed by Ferrell. It was produced around 1934. The bottom surfaces of it are glazed, but do not have any impressed or molded Roseville mark; some pieces occasionally retain an original Roseville sticker. The Laurel pattern exploits the telescoping technique to great advantage. The handles, decorative for the most part, telescope upward and outward, and often the vase itself owes the architecture of its shape to the telescoping technique. Laurel also has a design underlayer, which consists of four vertical lines carved symmetrically on each side deep into the pot. This design underlayer almost appears as a trellis over which the laurel leaves grow.

Very early pre-cursors of Laurel can be found in the pottery of Peters and Reed. One example, shown here, is essentially identical overall to the Roseville Laurel pattern designed by Ferrell much later.

There are three different types of colors applied to this pattern, called "green," "yellow," and "persimmon." The green type is decorated in four colors, green, sandy tan, dark brown for the branches, and violet for the berries. The glaze is a rich velvety matte, often containing large crystalline parts. The green color is similar to the green of Baneda, and certainly rivals it in beauty. The technique of color shading from light to dark in order to create the impression of light falling upon the vase [the 'blush'] is only used in the green-decorated variety of Laurel. Both the yellow and the persimmon are monochrome in their background color. The yellow or gold type of Laurel uses a deep yellow as the overall background color, with the leaves painted in brown, and the recesses and the interior of the vase in glossy black. The persimmon type of color decoration uses a brownish orange as the background color with the leaves painted in green and the recesses of the design [but not the vase interior] decorated in black. The green variety of Laurel, obviously a personal favorite among the three, represents the finest quality of middle-period Roseville; the yellow and persimmon colors, because of their unusual usage of the color black, have on the other hand a distinctly modern, Art Deco appearance. There exist beautiful trial glaze examples of this line, based upon model #672.

There is only one extant stockbook page for the Laurel pattern, but there must have been at least one other page. We have surmised--but not documented--the stock numbers for the candlesticks and for the console bowls, since they are not shown on the existing Roseville stockbook page, and our examples of them have all lost their crayon stock number marks on the bottom. It is possible, though unlikely, that there could be a wallpocket or additional shapes, but we have never seen such. How beautiful would be a green jardiniere and pedestal in this line, but it is quite unlikely that any such may exist.

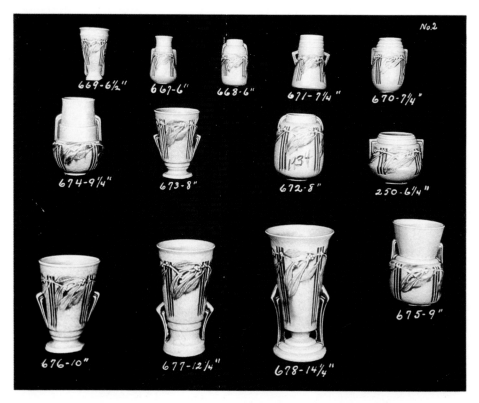

Figure. 143. The original Roseville stockbook catalogue for the Laurel pattern. At the top right hand corner it says 'No. 2' and we presume there may have been another page for the Laurel pattern. Photo courtesy of the Ohio Historical Society.

The shapes and model numbers for the pottery of the Laurel pattern are as follows:

RV Mold #	Type			
		#669-6.5	Vase	
		#670-7.25	Vase	
#15-2.5	Flower frog	#671-7.25	Vase	
#15-3.5	Flower frog	#672-8	Vase	
			Trial Glazes exist for #672-8	
#250-6.25	Bowl/rose bowl	#673-8	Vase	
#251-6.5	Console bowl [round]	#674-9.25	Vase	
#252-8	Console bowl [round]	#675-9	Vase	
#253-6.5	Console bowl [oblong]	#676-10	Vase	
#254-14	Console bowl [oblong]	#677-12.25	Vase	
		#678-14.5	Floor vase	
#667-6	Vase			
#668-6	Vase	#1094-4	Candlesticks [pair]	

Figure 144. A bowl designed by Ferrell [and signed in the mold] for Peters and Reed probably twenty years prior to the designs for Roseville. The similarity to the Roseville design is quite striking. This Peters and Reed bowl which has a deep brown glaze also may be found with a green glaze.

Figure 145. Two Laurel bowls, both decorated in green, models #251-6.5 and #252-8. These bowls differ only in their relative size, and if photographed apart they will appear identical in shape.

Figure 146. An oblong console bowl, #253-6.5, decorated in green.

Figure 147. A large oblong console bowl, Laurel model #254-14, in green. This design has gently scalloped edges.

Figure 148. The green Laurel candlesticks, model #1094-4. Telescoping is even used on these small objects to create the shape and the decorative handles.

Figure 159. Green Laurel vase, #670-7.25. Note the softened use of telescoping on all the vases shown on this page.

Figure 150. Green Laurel vase #667-6.

Figure 151. Green Laurel vase model #668-6.

Figure 152. Green Laurel vase model #669-6.5. This model is hard to find; its narrow base may have made it easily breakable.

Figure 153. Green Laurel vase #676-10; this model and #673-8 differ only in their relative sizes.

Figure 154. Green Laurel bowl #250-6.25

Figure 155. Green Laurel vase #672-8; this vase model was the one used for color trials.

Figure 156. Green Laurel vase #675-9.

Figure 157. Green Laurel vase model #673-8; it is a smaller size version of #676-10.

Figure 158. Persimmon Laurel vase #670-7.25. The use of black magnifies the effect of telescoping by highlighting it.

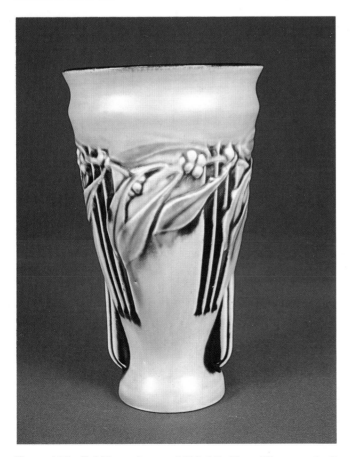

Figure 159. Gold Laurel vase, #669-6.5. How different esthetically the persimmon and gold versions are from the green.

Figure 160. Green Laurel vase model #674-9.25.

Figure 161. Green Laurel vase #671-7.25. Telescoping creates a sense of movement in this vase.

Figure 162. Persimmon Laurel vase #675-9.

Figure 163. Green Laurel vase #677-12.25. The beauty of the green glaze effects rivals that of Baneda.

Figure 164. Green Laurel vase #678-14.25. A spectacular piece of American art pottery.

Figure 165. Gold Laurel vase #674-9.25.

MONTACELLO

The Montacello pattern is closely related in its esthetic appeal to the Ferella line; it shares the symmetry of Ferella as well as its simplified decorative motifs. Also, both Montacello and Ferella used a spattered white overglaze. We know of no reason for the naming of this line as Montacello [recalling the family home of Thomas Jefferson but spelled differently], and we suspect the name may have been chosen simply because it has such a pleasing sound and noble connotation. To some people, there is a quality to this line that is consistent with the decorative arts of the American Southwest; although it is difficult to say with precision what this might be, it is possibly the simplicity of the round shapes as well as the abstract decorative motifs. The decoration of Montacello consists of one large band surrounded by two smaller bands around the upper part of the pot. There is then an abstract, stylized decorative motif symmetrically placed on the right and left sides of both front and back. In two cases, this decorative motif is based loosely on a flower, and in other cases it is merely abstract. There is a noticeable thickness to pots of the Montacello line when compared to lines such as Clemana or Morning Glory.

There is only one stockbook page for the Montacello pattern, and it appears to be the case that all but one model [#574-4, a budvase] are shown on that page. There are two color patterns for Montacello,

one called "tan," and the other "aqua." The exact color value of the aqua may be more blue in some cases and more green in others, but typically it is between the two. The tan pattern is decorated in four and sometimes five colors. The decorative motifs are painted in white and black, and yellow is sometimes used at the center of the motif. The narrow bands are in green around a center band of dark tan. The background color of the vase is light to dark tan with a mottled white overglaze that imparts an impressive texture to the pot. The aqua pattern uses a bluish green as the dominant background color, while the narrow bands are green, and the decorative motifs are again in black and white and sometimes an additional yellow. The colors from the decorative motifs often bleed downward onto the vase in a very pleasing way, but they do this to a very different extent on every pot, so that each pot is actually distinct from all other examples, as in the Baneda line. Some collectors like the pot to have substantial dripping of the color, while other collectors prefer the opposite. The candlesticks and the baskets in this pattern are particularly desirable and hard to locate. A flower frog is not listed for Montacello, but one presumably might exist. There does not at present appear to be any clearly dominant collector preference for one color over another, but such may emerge over time.

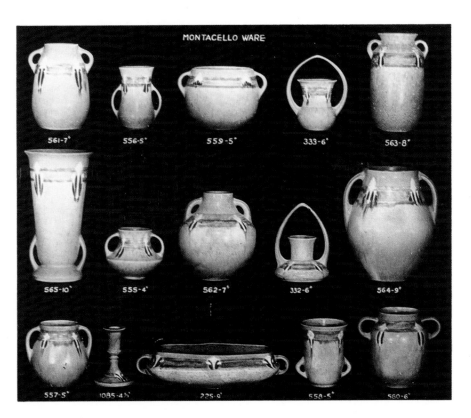

Figure. 166. The Roseville catalogue page for the Montacello pattern. The photograph shows all but one model, equally divided between tan and aqua. Photo courtesy of the Ohio Historical Society.

The pieces of the Montacello line are as follows. Note that #574-4 is discontinuous numerically with all the other models, and this piece also does not appear on the catalogue photograph.

RV Mold #	Type
#225-9	Console bowl
#332-6	Basket
#333-6	Basket
#555-4	Vase
#556-5	Vase
#557-5	Vase
#558-5	Vase
#559-5	Bowl
#560-6	Vase
#561-7	Vase
#562-7	Vase
#563-8	Vase
#564-9	Vase
#565-10	Vase
#574-4	Vase
#1084-5.5	Candlesticks

Figure 167. Montacello vase #563-8, in tan.

Figure 168. The decorative motif on #558-5. A minimum of five distinct colors had to be applied to decorate the pot.

Figure 169. Montacello vase #562-7 in tan.

Figure 170. Montacello miniature vase #555-4 in tan; this is possibly the most frequently seen piece of the entire line.

Figure 171. Montacello vase #574-4 in tan; this piece does not appear on the catalogue page for the pattern.

Figure 172. Montacello vase #556-5 in tan, similar in shape to one of the two baskets in the line.

Figure 173. Montacello vase #560-6 in tan.

Figure 174 [immediate right]. Montacello bowl #559-5 in tan.

Figure 175. [far right]. A closeup of the decorative motif used on this bowl.

Figure 176. Montacello console bowl #225-9.

Figure 177. The companion candlesticks to the bowl shown above, #1085-4.5, in tan.

Figure 178. A color trial version of Montacello model #558-5. The color is much more green than blue.

Figure 179. Montacello vase #558-5; a particularly nice example with rich texture.

Figure 180. Montacello vase #557-6 in tan.

Figure 181. Montacello vase #560-6 in aqua.

Figure 182. Montacello vase #564-9 in aqua.

Figure 183. Montacello vase #565-10, in aqua, the tallest piece of pottery in the line.

Figure 184. Montacello basket #332-6 in aqua.

Figure 185. Montacello basket #333-6 in aqua.

Figure 186. Montacello vase #561-7 in tan.

Figure 187. Montacello vase #565-10 in tan.

WINCRAFT

The Wincraft pattern was named after Robert Windisch, then president of the company. It is a superbly designed pattern, but it was not a great commercial success. The date for the production of Wincraft is 1948, in the post-war era when American taste was undergoing rapid and dramatic changes. The Wincraft pattern was an attempt by Roseville to come to terms with those changes. The Artwood pattern [described in *Volume 1*], thoroughly original in its design, also represented an attempt to keep in step with this post-war change in taste. In the lucrative American post-war market a deluge of inexpensive imported goods began to decrease the sales of Roseville pottery. Many of these were from the Orient, and popular decorative motifs at the time were things like Oriental dancers [in pajama-like costumes with exotic hats], sleek black panthers, palm trees, and miniature squat Oriental trees. During the 1950's these motifs were used on countless lamps, wall ornaments, decorative prints, curtains, rugs, upholstery and everything else that could be used to decorate the home. Popular colors at that time were aqua, coral, turquoise, chartreuse, and bright, glossy gold. In essence, then, the 1950's culture and taste amounted to almost an antithesis of everything that the middle-period of Roseville pottery represented.

Frank Ferrell, as interviewed by Norris Schneider in the late 1950's, stated with great pride that he had never copied anything in his long artistic career until asked to do so for this modern line by Robert Windisch. It is probable that Ferrell may have been asked by his employer to incorporate a panther motif into the line, since the panther was a decorative fad with rampant popularity at that time. An unusual unglazed model of the panther motif carved by Frank Barks is shown here. It is interesting that the Wincraft vase with the panther bears the stock #290-11--a model number whose heigth is out of sequence with previous numbers--which probably means that the vase was added after the enitre line had already been designed. In the popular decorative arts of the 1950's were planters shaped as panthers, TV lights, table lamps, decorative figurines, drapes, wall decorations, and so forth. But in all these depictions, the panther is usually seen from the side, walking or running. Ferrell and Barks did create a panther motif, but their panther is altogether different and not a copy of anything. It is seen as if from an aerial view, with the panther jumping from out of a tree.

Although the Wincraft line was not successful as a commercial entity, it is entirely possible that it might have been. Roseville was most famous for its soft

Figure. 188. The original model of the panther motif hand-carved by Frank Barks. It is shown in this photograph on its side, whereas on the vase, Model #290-11, it appears in mid-leap, coming down out of a tree. The clay base on which it is carved is more than one inch thick. Note the beautiful curvature to the entire design, and how greatly it differs from other depictions of panthers common on the many mass-produced lamps and figurines of the 1950's era.

velvet-like glaze; it could be convincingly argued that the lustrous matte glazes developed by Roseville were an important ingredient in the overall commercial success of the pottery. Frank Ferrell in fact wanted Wincraft to be executed in just such a matte glaze [Schneider, 1957]. But Windisch, eager for a dramatic turnaround in sales, disagreed, and the line was brought forth to the public with the deepest glass-like finish ever made by Roseville or perhaps any pottery company. Many pieces of Wincraft literally look like pottery encased in a sheet of glass, just as in the manner of what is called cased glass. Retailers purchased Wincraft the first time that the salesmen came around with it, since they were used to buying Roseville, but the second time they balked and refused to buy it, pointing out that this was not the Roseville they knew. Salesmen would put Roseville stickers right on top of each piece, easily visible to the customer, but even this did no good. The public did not recognize it as Roseville and they would not buy it. However, there are many experimental pieces of Wincraft [and its companion pattern Artwood] that were made with a soft, matte glaze; these pieces are especially beautiful, and probably give us a better idea of how Ferrell would have liked the line to have been executed. One can only wonder whether the life span of the Roseville Pottery might have been extended had Ferrell's artistic instincts been heeded.

What makes the Wincraft line so artistically interesting is the dramatically different shapes of so many of the pieces. The Wincraft line used many of the floral motifs that had been used with great success on other Roseville lines: pinecone and pine needles, dogwood, white rose, teasel, and even perhaps the tulips one finds in Futura. It also uses a variety of other plants never seen before in Roseville, such as cactus, geranium, ivy, wheat and a number of different leaves and wildflowers.

The colors used to decorate the Wincraft line reflect the influence of the taste and style of the 1950's. Wincraft was decorated in three color lines, called by Roseville Apricot, Azure Blue, and Chartreuse. There are five Roseville stockbook pages for Wincraft, which were originally published in black and white in the first edition of Henzke's *Art Pottery of America* [1982]. In 1995 we purchased these from her and we show them here in color. These pages are quite interesting because they show many of the pieces in an indisputably matte finish. In other words, many of these pieces photographed for these pages were probably very early color-trial examples. Many of the color trials [found without a high-gloss glaze] will be found to have different model numbers on the bottom. For example, #208-8 is a basket; an identically-shaped pot with a trial glaze has model #2BK-8 on the bottom. Another interesting oddity is Model #253, a triple candleholder. This model was redesigned as shown in this book, possibly because the original design may have been difficult to mold.

The Apricot line of Wincraft is decorated in three and often four colors, depending on the particular model. Each pot is dark brown at the bottom which shades pleasingly to a rich golden tan. The Azure Blue line shades from a deep navy blue at the bottom to a piercing rich aqua color for most of the vase. The Chartreuse line is also dark brown at the base and light green higher up. In each line, flowers or leaves may appear in white, yellow, or green, or with berries in red. On many pieces of all color lines, there is a mottled white overglaze which adds depth and texture to each pot. We have not encountered any flower frogs in this line. All pieces are glazed on the bottom and have the word Roseville and the appropriate model number and dimension on each piece. There would appear to be some collector preference at the present time for the Azure Blue line of Wincraft, but all three color lines are found in roughly equal representation on the antiques marketplace, and collector preferences have created differences in price among them in some cases. While some of the Wincraft models are easily found in the antiques marketplace, a great number of them are very, very difficult to locate. Model #233, a console bowl of gigantic proportions is seldom seen today. Also, there is a very large and beautiful basket decorated with a cactus and its flower which embodies Ferrell's technique superbly; this basket is rarely seen today in undamaged condition.

Had the Roseville Pottery survived as a commercial and artistic enterprise, the Wincraft line gives us a hint of what might have emerged as lines for the late 1950's and beyond: Ivy, Tulip, Geranium, Oak, Wheat, Cactus, Wild Grape, and possibly modern versions of Dogwood and Pinecone.

Figure 189. A Wincraft jardiniere, in azure blue, model #257-6.

The different pots of the Wincraft pattern are enumerated here below. There are probably more different utilitarian items in this line than in any other made by Roseville. Many of these pieces can be easily found in the antique marketplace, whereas others are seen only very rarely. There are some inconsistencies in these model numbers, and as elsewhere in this book, spaces between the numbers indicate a discontinuity. Early numbers found on trial glaze pots are shown in parentheses, i.e., 2PT = #256-5, where the letters indicate pot, flower holder, tankard, basket, and vase.

RV Mold #	Type
#208-8	Basket
#209-12	Basket
#210-12	Basket
#216-8 [=2TK-8]	Ewer/budvase
#217-6	Ewer/budvase
#218-18	Floor ewer
#221-8	Cornucopia
#222-8	Cornucopia
#226-8	Console bowl round
#227-10	Console bowl
#228-12	Console bowl
#229-14	Console bowl
#230-7	Tray
#231-10	Bowl
#232-12	Nut dish
#233-14	Console bowl
#240-B	Covered box
#240-T	Ashtray
#241	Rose bowl/Vase
#242-8	Ball vase

#250-P	Coffee/chocolate pot
#250-C	Creamer
#250-S	Sugar bowl
#251-3 [=2CS1]	Candlesticks
#252-4	Candlesticks
#253	Triple Candlesticks
#256-5 [=2PT]	Flowerpot/Jardiniere
#257-6	Footed Jardiniere
#259	Bookends
#261-6	Hanging Basket
#263-14	Floorvase
#266-4	Wallpocket
#267-5	Wallpocket
#268-12	Windowbox
#271-P	Teapot
#271-C	Creamer
#271-S	Sugar bowl Set
#272-6	Vase fan
#273-8 [=2FH-8]	Vase fan
#274-7	Vase rectangular
#275-12	Vase fan
#281-6	Budvase
#282-8	Vase
#283-8 [=2V2-8]	Vase
#284-10	Vase
#285-10 [=2V2-10]	Vase
#286-12	Vase
#287-12	Vase
#288-15	Vase
#289-18	Floorvase
#290-11	Vase [panther]

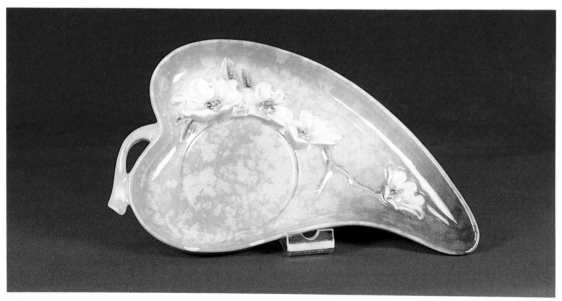

Figure190. Wincraft tray, model #230-7, in apricot; the indented circle was probably meant for a cup.

WINCRAFT *by Roseville* ZANESVILLE, OHIO

242   210   274

232   290   231

218   275   263

Each item available in three distinctive colors:
Apricot—Azure Blue—Chartreuse

Figure 191. Page 2-A, one of five catalogue pages for the Wincraft pattern. This page for some reason has some of the most desirable pieces. Many of the vases appear to be done in a matte, rather than glossy, finish. Model #253 has not been seen by the author in the precise design shown on page 1-A.

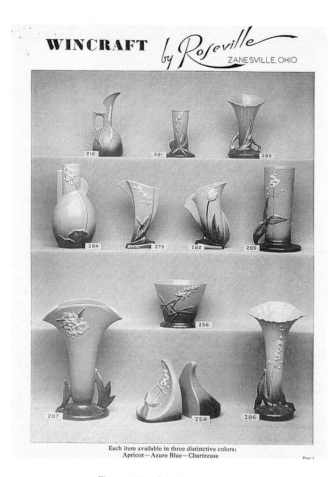

Figure 192. Catalogue page 1.

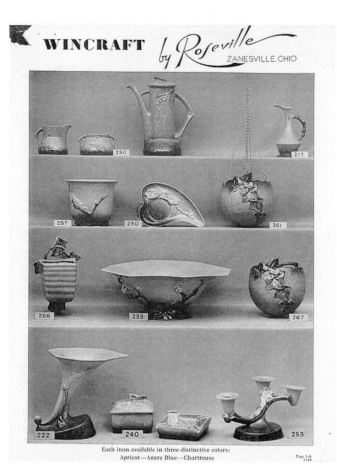

Figure 193. Catalogue page 1A.

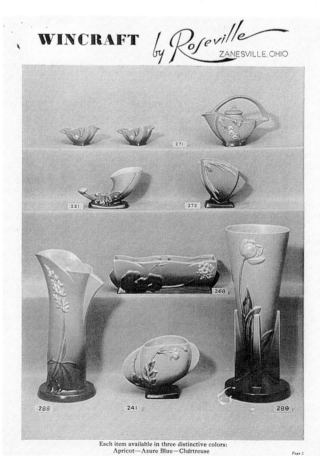

Figure 194. Catalogue page 2.

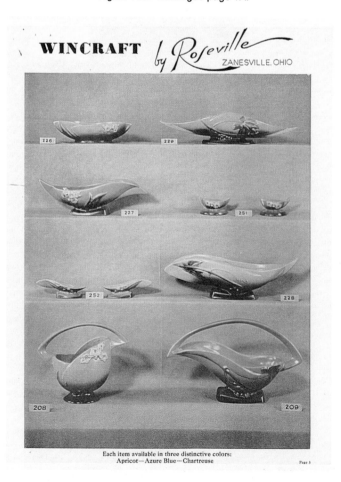

Figure 195. Catalogue page 3.

Figure 196. A boat-form console bowl in chartreuse, model #231-10. It uses a teasel motif for decoration, and the ends of the bowl are elegantly telescoped upward and outward.

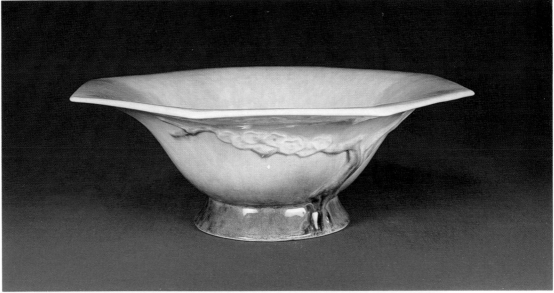

Figure 197. An octagonal console bowl, model #233-14, of very massive proportions, in chartreuse; its outer diameter is just short of 14".

Figure 198. Pair of bookends, model #259, in chartreuse; the free-form shape is suggested by the leaf of the wildflower depicted upon it.

Figure 199. A pair of triple candlesticks, model #253, in chartreuse. Note that these are noticeably different in shape from the model depicted on the catalogue page.

Figure 200. An elegant boat-form bowl, model #232-12; it is extremely narrow and long, and almost appears to *be* the leaf it portrays.

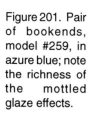

Figure 201. Pair of bookends, model #259, in azure blue; note the richness of the mottled glaze effects.

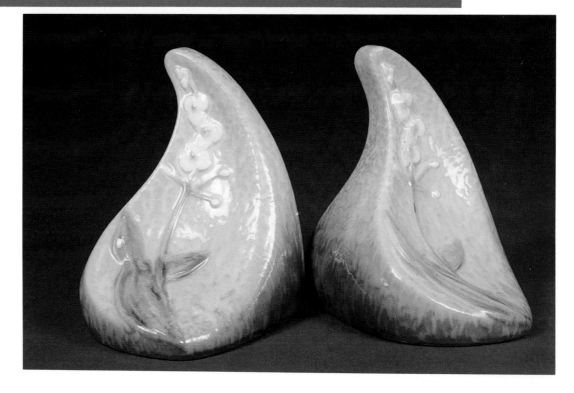

Figure 202. A planter or a jardiniere, model #256-5, in apricot. This photograph shows the reverse side of the pot which has fewer leaves than on the front.

Figure 203. A planter, model #256, in a trial color and glaze that has a pink hue to it; the glaze is a semi-matte and there is a lot of texture and color variation in it. It is marked on the bottom #2PT.

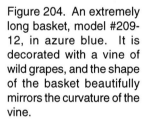

Figure 204. An extremely long basket, model #209-12, in azure blue. It is decorated with a vine of wild grapes, and the shape of the basket beautifully mirrors the curvature of the vine.

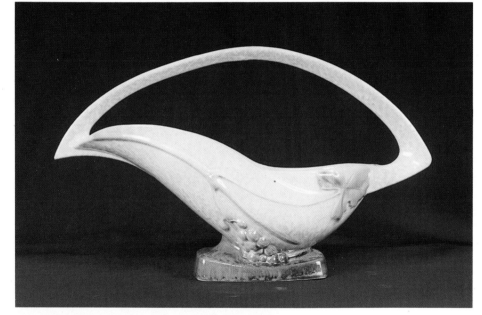

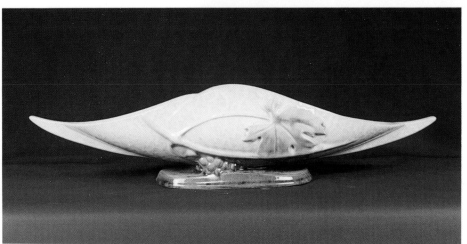

Figure 205. A very elongated console bowl, also decorated with a wild grape motif, in azure blue. This is model #229-14, and because of its size it is not often seen. It would certainly harmonize well with the streamlined furniture that became popular in the 1950's.

Figure 206. Wincraft console bowl #227-10, in azure blue, decorated with a cluster of small white flowers, possibly phlox, which grows abundantly in traditional gardens.

Figure 207. Wincraft model #226-8, in azure blue; this round console bowl appears to open like a flower, and like model #227-10, it is also decorated with small white flowers.

Figure 208. The bottom of model #285-10 with the raised Roseville signature. The bottom is covered in glaze, and the base was ground [at the time of production] so that it will stand straight.

Figure 209. The bottom of the same model vase as shown in Figure 208, but on a color trial. The raised model number is "2V2-10" and the numbers below it refer to colors/glazes used on it.

Figure 210. A coffee or chocolate set with a covered pot, creamer, and sugar, in apricot, model #250P, #250C, and #250S. Note that only the pot was made with a cover. It is beautifully decorated with a wild berry motif.

Figure 211. Wincraft console bowl model #228-12, in apricot, decorated with a vine of wild grapes.

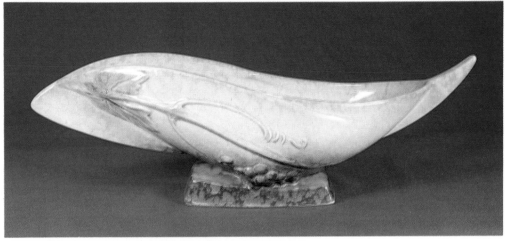

Figure 212. A beautifully designed bowl for roses, Wincraft model #241, in apricot. The shape is created by two ovals, one inside the other, with the top of the outer one being truncated. It seems really to float upon its pedestal. The rose was an atypical choice of a flower for decoration, but it may have been irresistible given the function of the vase.

Figure 213. A Wincraft cornucopia, #221-8, in apricot. The spare decorative motif is that of wild grapes.

Figure 214. Wincraft round wallpocket #267-5, in apricot. The hanging basket and both wallpockets of the Wincraft pattern use ivy, an ever-popular houseplant, as the decorative motif. As is frequently the case in the Wincraft pattern, the pot depicts the plant which it most likely will contain. But for this smart piece to decorate a wall, there is almost no need for it to have a plant. The back of the wallpocket is of course flat, and other than that, the only design difference of note between this model and the hanging basket is the small branch of ivy twig that is found on the right side of this model.

Figure 215. A covered box and ashtray, model #240-B and #240-T, in azure blue. These pieces use a modernized version of the dogwood motif, a motif used by Ferrell since the 1920's and probably earlier.

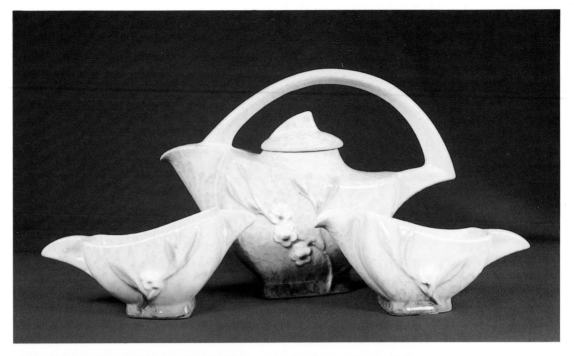

Figure 216. Wincraft tea set #271P, #271C, and #271S, in azure blue; only the pot is made with a cover. The teapot is beautifully curved, and this curvilinear design is carried over to the creamer and sugar.

Figure 217. Wincraft candlesticks model #251-3, in azure blue, which could accompany either of two console bowls decorated with the same white flowers.

Figure 218. Wincraft candlesticks model #252-4, in azure blue, which could accompany either of two console bowls decorated with grapevine.

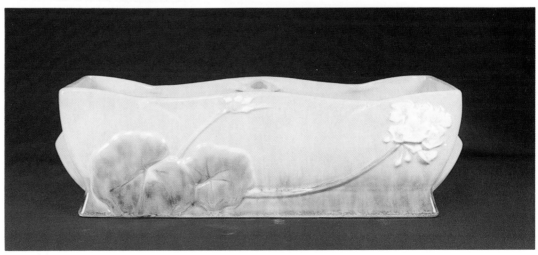

Figure 219. Wincraft model #268-12, a windowbox planter, in azure blue. This piece is decorated with geraniums, which may well be the plant its designers thought would most often be placed in it.

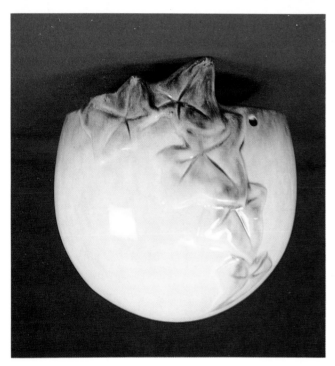

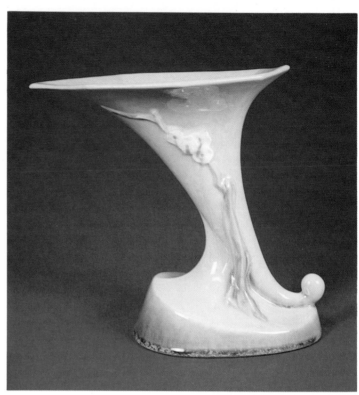

Figure 220. Wincraft hanging basket, model #261-6, in azure blue; it is slightly larger than the wallpocket of similar design.

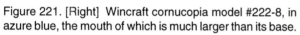

Figure 221. [Right] Wincraft cornucopia model #222-8, in azure blue, the mouth of which is much larger than its base.

Figure 222. Wincraft fan vase, #273-8, in azure blue. Note the white mottled overglaze which gives texture to the pot.

Figure 223. The same model, #273-8, as shown in Figure 222, but in a matte finish trial color of greenish yellow and brown. However, the mold numbers on the bottom are #2FH-8.

Figure 224. Wincraft vase model #284-10 in apricot. The use of geometric motifs and of asymmetry give this vase its character.

Figure 225. Wincraft vase #287-12 in azure blue; the design has been simplified so that the flowers have no stem.

Figure 226. A Wincraft budvase, #281-6, in azure blue. Compare its geometric motifs with that of the vase just above, #284-10.

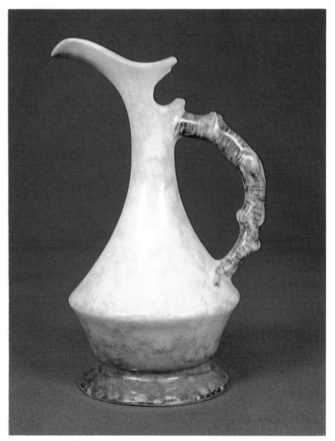

Figure 227. Wincraft model #217-6, in apricot. This miniature ewer, with its twig handle, was to be used as a budvase.

Figure 228. Wincraft vase #285-10, in azure blue. Note the original way the flower becomes an organic part of the vase.

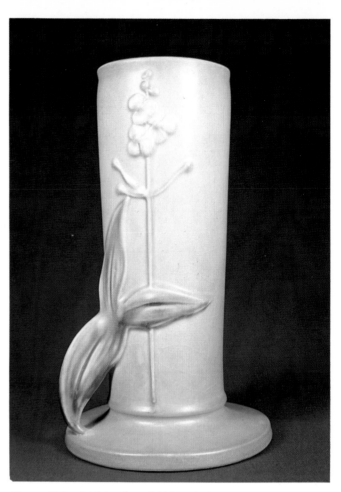

Figure 229. A trial color of #285-10, in tan and yellow with a matte finish; it is marked #2V2-10.

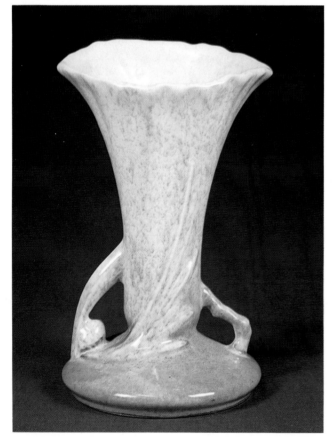

Figure 230. Wincraft vase model #283-8, but in a trial color, a pinkish gray. Its mold number is #2V2-8.

Figure 231. Wincraft vase model #283-8, but in a trial color, a mottled peach and brown. Its mold number is #2V2-8.

Figure 232. A trial color of #285-10, in peach and brown with a a gray leaf and a matte finish; it is marked #2V2-10.

Figure 233. A trial color of #285-10, in light green and brown with a matte finish, marked #2V2-10. Note the dark green leaf.

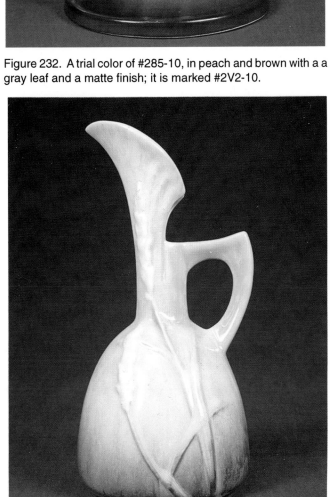

Figure 234. A Wincraft ewer/budvase, #216-8, in chartreuse. The color and glaze are very rich, with hints of aqua and pink.

Figure 235. Wincraft budvase, model #281-6, in chartreuse.

Figure 237. A rectangular vase with a non-floral decoration, model #274-7, in chartreuse.

Figure 236. Wincraft vase #282-8, in chartreuse. Note how telescoping has created a vase that seems to move upward.

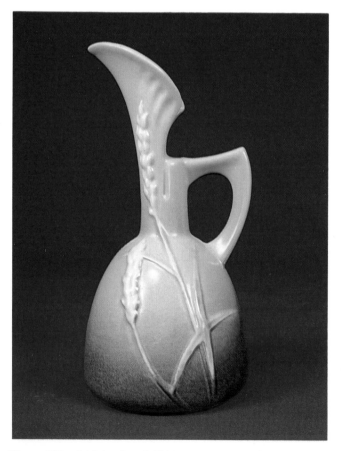

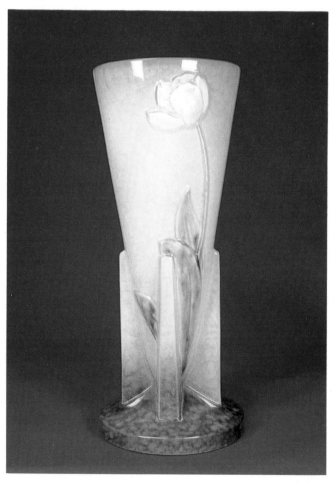

Figure 238. A trial color of #216-8, in peach and brown with a matte finish; it is marked #2TK-8.

Figure 239. A massive Wincraft floorvase, #289-18, in apricot. The buttress handles and the single tulip remind one of Futura.

Figure 240. A rectangular vase with a non-floral decoration, model #274-7, in azure blue.

Figure 241. Wincraft vase model #272-6, in azure blue, a modern version of Ferrell's favorite motif.

Figure 242. A Wincraft wallpocket, model #266-4, in azure blue.

Figure 243. Wincraft vase #275-12, in azure blue, one of the most beautiful models in the entire line.

Figure 244. Wincraft basket #208-8, in azure blue.

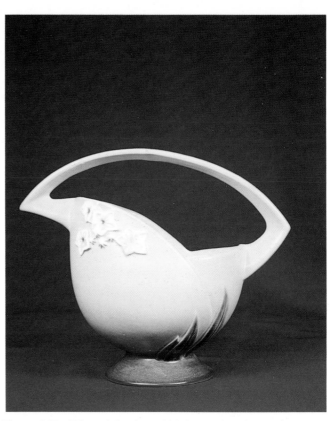

Figure 245. Wincraft basket #208-8, a color trial similar to the standard, but with a matte glaze. Note the missing flower stem.

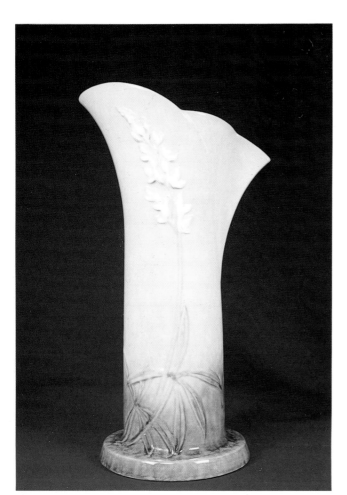

Figure 246. Wincraft vase #288-15 in azure blue.

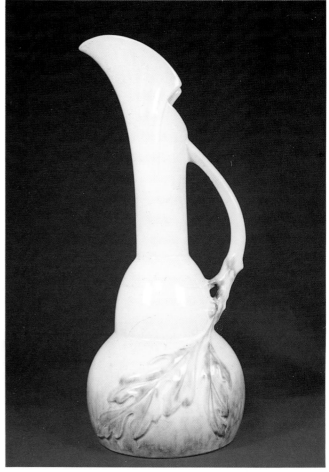

Figure 247. A very large size Wincraft ewer, in azure blue, model #218-18.

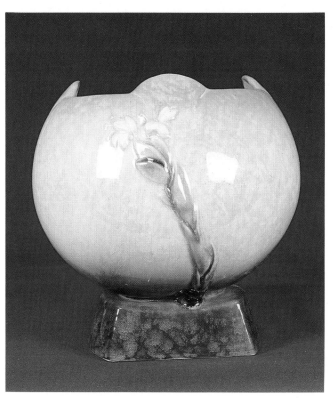

Figure 248. Wincraft ball vase #242-8, in apricot; this is possibly one of the largest ball vases ever made by Roseville.

Figure 249. Wincraft vase #242-8, as seen from the back. It depicts a kind of flowering shrub from the American Southwest.

Figure 250. Wincraft vase #287-12, in apricot; because there is no stem, the flowers appear almost as a corsage.

Figure 251. A massive Wincraft floorvase, #263-14, in apricot. It uses a modern version of dogwood, with twig handles. Note the unusual telescoped buttress near the base.

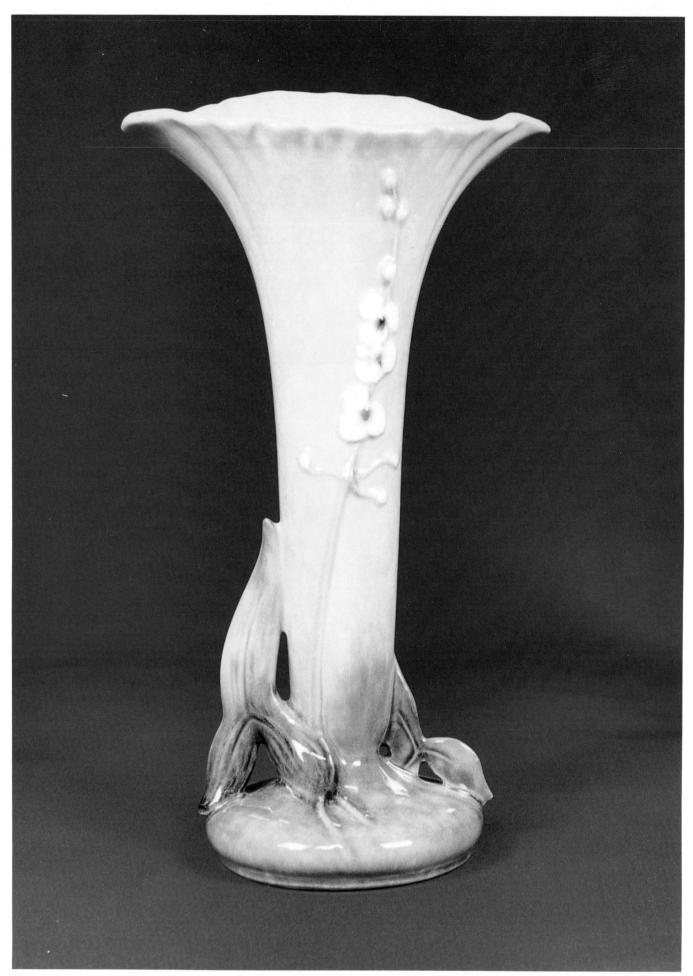

Figure 252. Azure blue Wincraft vase, model #286-12. Note how the wildflower has become incorporated into the vase.

Figure 253. Wincraft vase #275-12, in apricot. A superb example of the use of telescoping to create a dynamic shape.

Figure 254. Wincraft vase #290-11, in apricot. This is Ferrell's accomodation to 1950's taste.

Figure 255. Wincraft basket #210-12, in chartreuse; a cactus and its flower are the floral motif.
Note how telescoping has been used to create the handle.